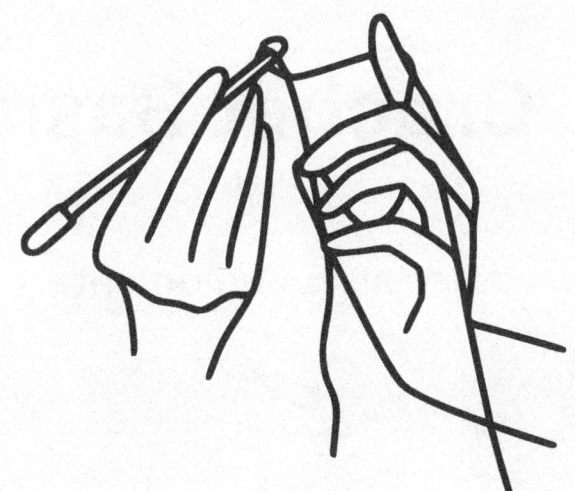

CROCHET DOG SWEATER PATTERNS

Stylish Dog Sweater Patterns for Every Pup

| 1 | Introduction |

CHAPTER I.

| 2 | **Crochet Basics** |

3	Materials & Equipments
10	Stitches & Techniques
38	Abbreviation

CHAPTER II.

42 Crochet Dog Sweaters Patterns

1	Dandy Dog Sweater	43
2	Large Dog Sweater	52
3	Striped Dog Coat	62
4	Houndstooth Dog Sweater	67
5	Fab Dog Coat	72
6	Beginner Dog Coat	76
7	Granny Square Dog Sweater	80
8	Textured Dog Coat	84
9	Purpleicious Dog Coat	89

Introduction

Welcome to "Crochet Dog Sweaters Patterns: Cozy Creations for Your Canine Companion." If you're a crochet enthusiast with a love for dogs, this book is your gateway to combining your crafting skills with your affection for your furry friends. Within these pages, you'll find a collection of charming and practical sweater patterns that will keep your dogs snug and stylish in all seasons.

In the first section, "Crochet Basics," we'll ensure you're well-prepared to embark on your crocheting journey. Covering everything from essential materials and equipment to fundamental stitches and techniques, you'll have a solid foundation to create these adorable and functional sweaters. The included abbreviations guide will be your handy reference as you work through the patterns.

As you delve into the heart of the book, "Crochet Dog Sweaters Patterns," you'll discover an array of designs catering to various sizes and styles. From the dapper Dandy Dog Sweater to the chic Houndstooth Dog Sweater, each pattern has been meticulously crafted to offer comfort and charm to your canine companions. Whether you're a crochet novice or an experienced crafter, you'll find joy in creating personalized garments that keep your dogs warm and showcase your love for both crochet and your furry friends. Let's embark on this creative journey together, crafting cozy canine couture one stitch at a time.

CHAPTER I.

Crochet Basics

Materials & Equipment

Yarn

Yarns are available in a variety of weights. Weight refers to the thickness of the strand and fiber contents. Yarn comes in either a long center-pull skein or a ball. The weight of the skein or ball and the total yardage is determined by the weight of the strand of yarn.

There are six standard yarn weight groups determined by the Craft Yarn Council of America, and the weights are denoted with a number and symbol. (see the table on the next page.)

Yarn Weight Symbol & Category Names	1 Super Fine	2 Fine	3 Light	4 Medium	5 Bulky	6 Super Bulky
Type of Yarns in Category	Sock, Fingering, Baby	Sport, Baby	DK, Light Worsted	Worsted, Afghan, Aran	Chunky, Craft, Rug	Bulky, Roving
Knit Gauge Range* in Stockinette Stitch to 4 inches	27–32 sts	23–26 sts	21–24 sts	16–20 sts	12–15 sts	6–11 sts
Recommended Needle in Metric Size Range	2.25–3.25 mm	3.25–3.75 mm	3.75–4.5 mm	4.5–5.5 mm	5.5–8 mm	8 mm and larger
Recommended Needle U.S. Size Range	1 to 3	3 to 5	5 to 7	7 to 9	9 to 11	11 and larger
Crochet Gauge* Ranges in Single Crochet to 4 inch	21–32 sts	16–20 sts	12–17 sts	11–14 sts	8–11 sts	5–9 sts
Recommended Hook in Metric Size Range	2.25–3.5 mm	3.5–4.5 mm	4.5–5.5 mm	5.5–6.5 mm	6.5–9 mm	9 mm and larger
Recommended Hook U.S. Size Range	B–1 to E–4	E–4 to 7	7 to I–9	I–9 to K–10½	K–10½ to M–13	M–13 and larger

Keep the ball bands from yarn to use as reference. Pin the band to the gauge swatch and keep them both together with any remaining yarn from the project. Also include spare buttons and any extra trim used in the project, and tuck everything in a labeled zip-close plastic bag. This way, you'll be able to check the washing instructions of the yarn, and you'll always have extra materials on hand for repairs.

Thread

Threads are also available in several weights with varying ounces or yards per ball. Most crochet threads are made of 100% cotton fiber. The most popular and widely available thread weight is size 10, often still referred to as "bedspread-weight cotton", which is used for all types of lace projects such as doilies and table runners. The higher the thread size number, the finer the thread: Size 20 is finer than Size 10, and Sizes 30 and 40 are finer still. Yarns and threads are available in many different thicknesses, twists and finishes.

Crochet Hook

First, if you are new to crocheting, a crochet hook is a handheld tool that helps create crochet stitches (loops of yarn) with yarn. Crochet hooks come in many sizes, and are made of different materials and varieties. Hooks are one of the first crochet supplies along with yarn you will want to get.

Most sizes of crochet hooks are labeled on the thumb area of the hook, which is actually the diameter of the shaft of the hook in mm. Occasionally, you may hear them referred to as a crochet needle, but they are actually called crochet hooks.

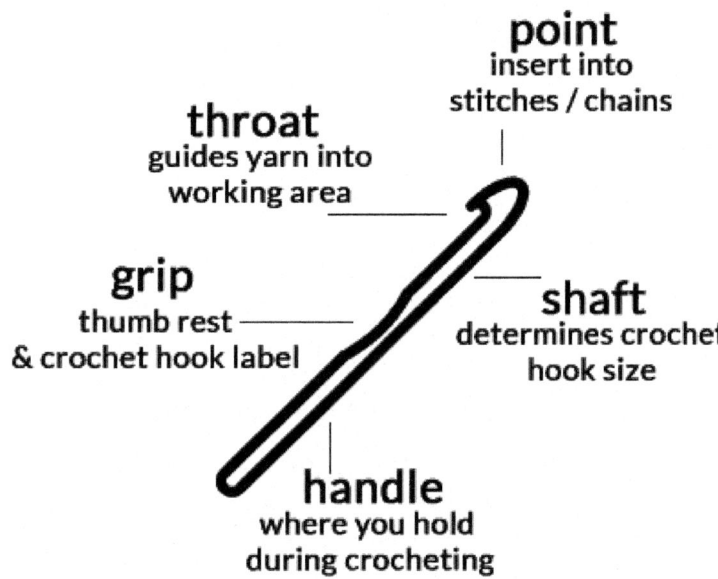

Anatomy of a Crochet Hook:

- **Throat** – The part of the hook that guides yarn into the working area of the project.

- **Point** – Insert this part of the crochet hook into chains and stitches.

- **Grip** – This part includes the thumb rest and the label indicating which size the hook is.

- **Shaft** – This part of the crochet hook determines the hook size. The size of the shaft determines the size of the yarn loops.

- **Handle** – This is where you hold the hook while you crochet.

Take a look at the image above that shows all the parts of a crochet hook and what they are used for during crocheting.

Crochet Hook Size

The size of a crochet hook corresponds to specific weights of yarn, and crochet patterns usually list a suggested hook size to help you make the pattern as close to the original design as possible. Yarn labels also list a hook size or range of sizes that are recommended to work with that particular yarn.

One thing to be aware of is that crochet hook sizes are not completely standardized. Because crochet has evolved as a folk art over time, and across continents, hook sizes have evolved separately as well. Crochet hooks can be measured in either letters (US) or metric units (UK). Most yarn labels will use one or both types of crochet hook measurements, but there are times when you have to convert the size yourself to make sure you are using the recommended hook size.

Crochet Hook Size Chart (US&UK)

Metric	US	UK	Metric	US	UK
2 mm	0	14	6 mm	J-10	4
2.25 mm	B-1	13	6.50 mm	K- 10 1/2	3
2.75 mm	C-2	12	7 mm		2
3 mm		11	7.50 mm		1
3.25 mm	D-3	10	8 mm	L-11	0
3.50 mm	E-4		9 mm	M/N-13	00
3.75 mm	F-5	9	10 mm	N/P-15	000
4 mm	G-6	8	12 mm	O	
4.25 mm	GBoye		15 mm	P/Q	
4.50 mm	7	7	16 mm	Q	
5 mm	H-8	6	25 mm	T/U/X	
5.50 mm	I-9	5	30 mm	T/X	

Other equiments

In addition to a crochet hook, you will need a bluntended yarn needle for darning in yarn ends. Other essentials include scissors, pins, and a tape measure.

Handy extras such as stitch markers and row counters will help keep track of stitches

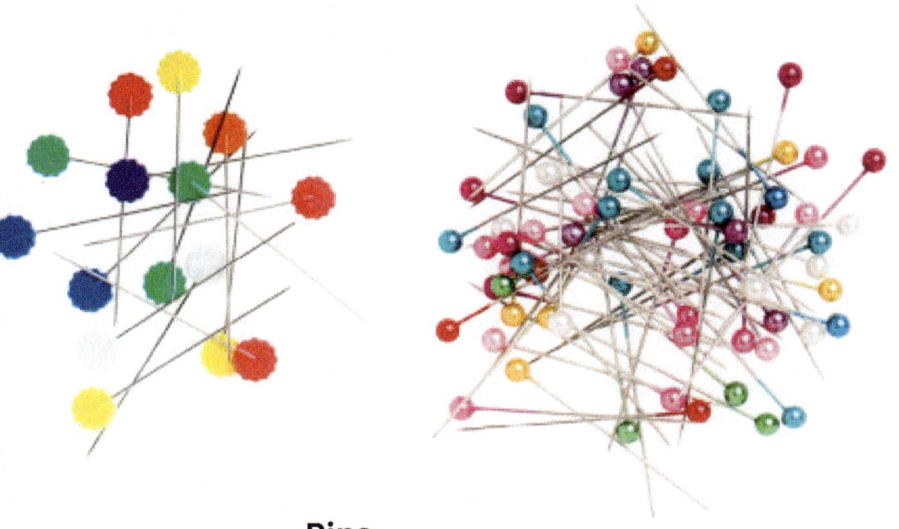

Blunt-ended yarn needles
Use these for sewing seams and darning in yarn ends. (Make sure the eye of the needle is big enough for your chosen yarn.)

Pins
Use pins with large heads for aiding seaming and blocking

Tape measure
Keep a tape measure on hand for checking your gauge and measuring your crochet.

Scissors

Keep a sharp pair of scissors on hand for cutting yarn and trimming off yarn ends.

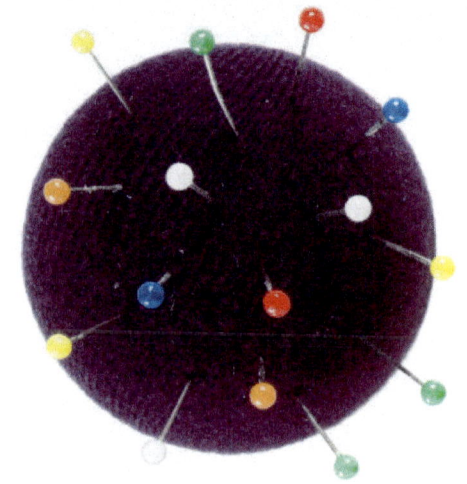

Pin cushion

A useful item to have by your side when working.

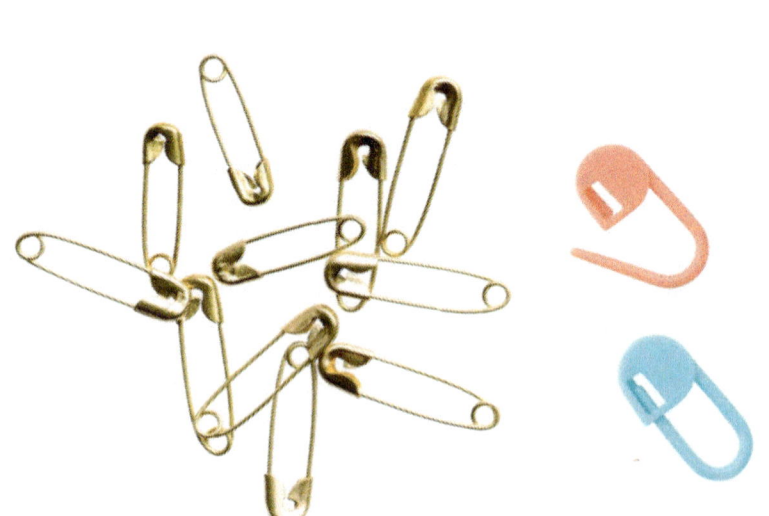

Stitch markers

These can be hooked onto the crochet to mark a specific row or a specific stitch in the row, or to mark the right side of your crochet.

Row counter

These are useful for keeping track of where you are in your crochet. String on a length of cotton yarn and hang it around your neck—change it each time you complete a row.

Stitches & Techniques

Holding the Hook

There are different ways of holding the crochet hook. You will need to experiment and find the way that feels the most comfortable for you. If your hand isn't comfortable, it will cause your hand to cramp up, and your stitches will not be even. We will show you two ways to hold the hook. Again, play around and find the one that feels most natural to you.

The first position is similar to holding a pencil. Hold the crochet hook as you would a pencil with your thumb and index finger on the finger hold, and the third finger near the tip of the hook.

The second position is similar to holding a knife, and your hand will grip over the hook. Place your hand over the crochet hook with the handle resting against the palm of your hand and your thumb and third finger gripping the thumb rest.

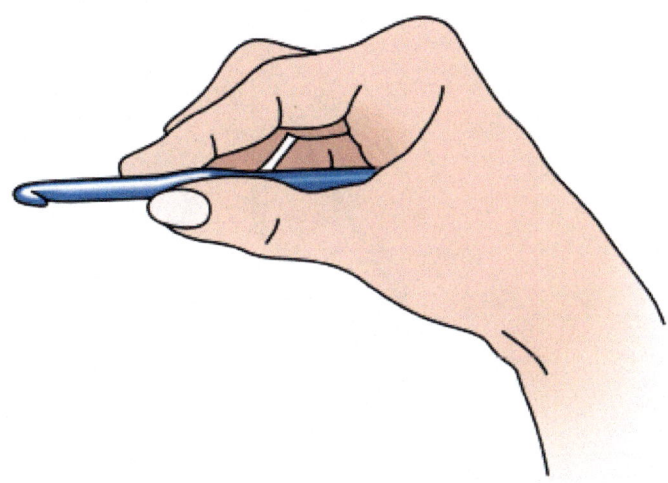

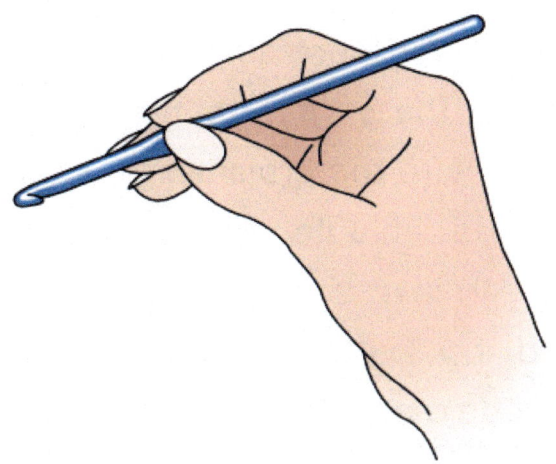

The crochet hook should be turned slightly toward you, not facing up or down. The crochet hook should be held firmly, but not tightly. At first you will find yourself gripping tightly but over time, once you feel more comfortable, you will find your hand relaxes.

Holding the Yarn

To maintain the slight tension in the yarn necessary for easy, even stitches, you may find it helpful to wrap the yarn around the fingers of the hand opposite the one holding the hook. Try one of these ways, or find another way that feels comfortable to you.

In the illustration below, the left hand holds your crochet work and at the same time controls the tension of the yarn. The left-hand middle finger is used to manipulate the yarn, while the index finger and thumb hold on to the work.

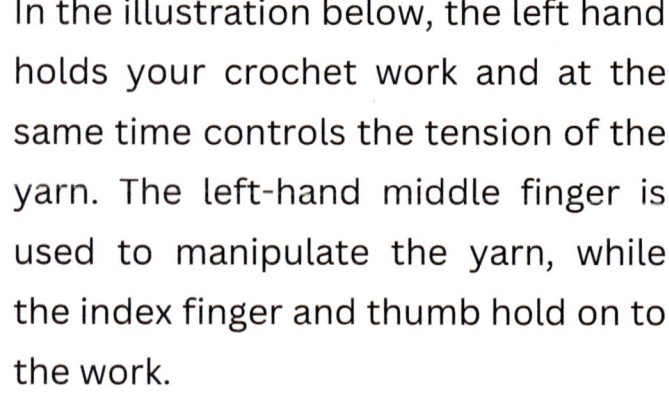

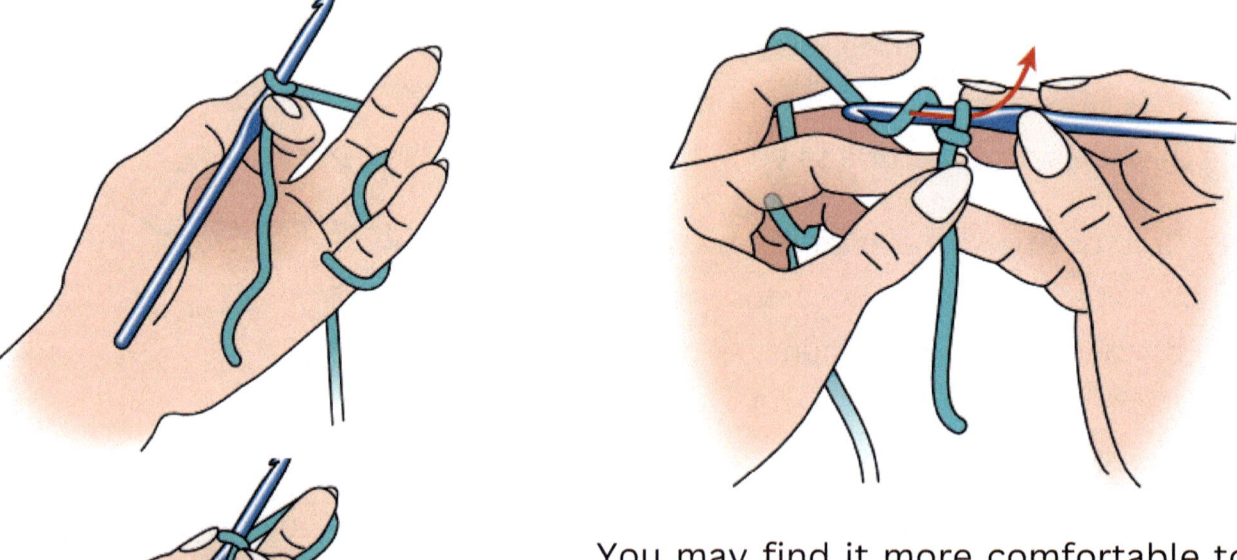

You may find it more comfortable to manipulate the yarn with the index finger and hold the project with your thumb and middle finger. While you're learning, if one ways feels awkward, try another way until you find the one that suits you.

Foundation Chain

Almost all crochet begins with a base or foundation chain, which is a series of chain stitches, beginning with a slip knot

Slip Knot

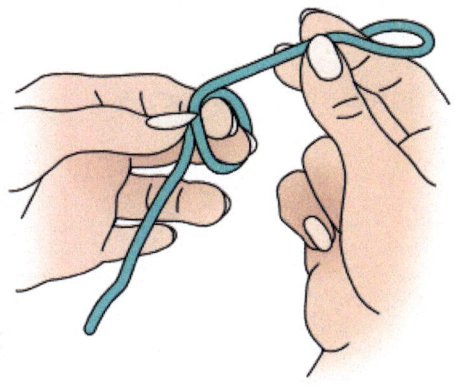

1. Make a circle with yarn or thread

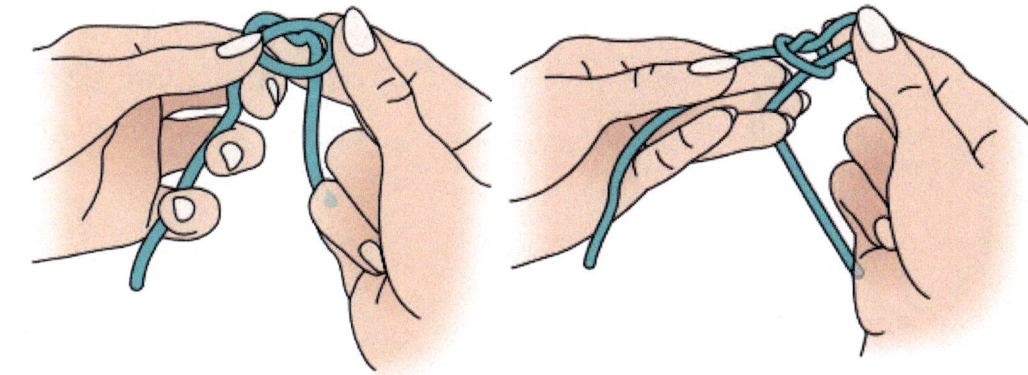

2. Pull a loop through the circle.

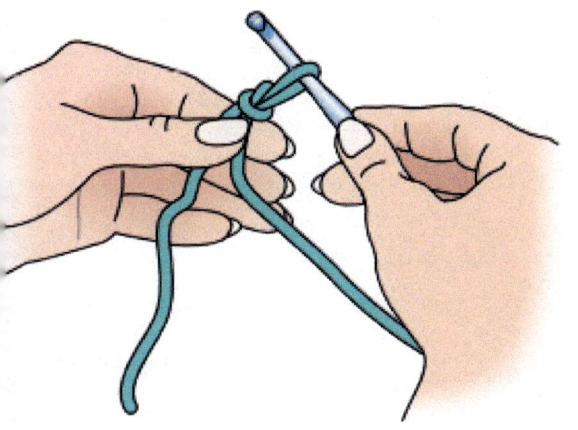

3. Insert the hook in the loop

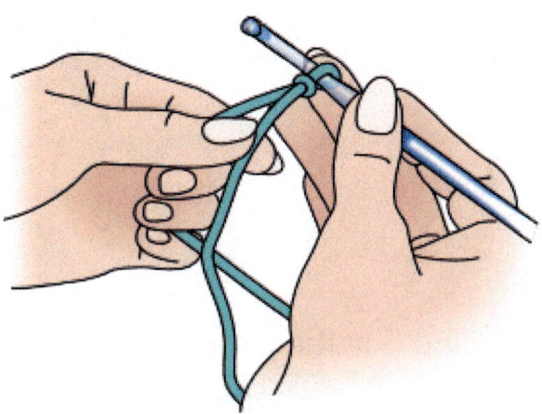

4. Pull gently and evenly to tighten the loop and slide the knot up to the hook.

Foundation Chain

Yarn Over (yo)

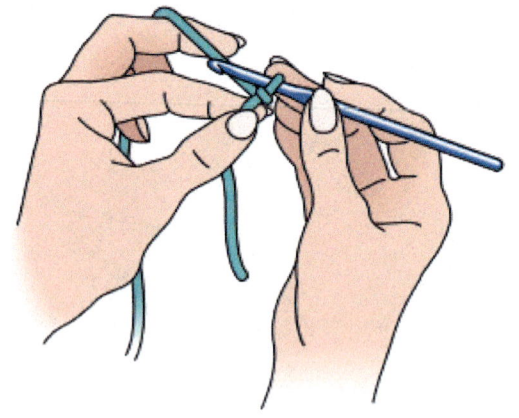

Wrap the yarn from back to front over the hook (or hold the yarn still and maneuver the hook). This movement of the yarn over the hook is used over and over again in crochet and is usually called "yarn over", abbreviated as "yo".

Chain Stitch (ch)

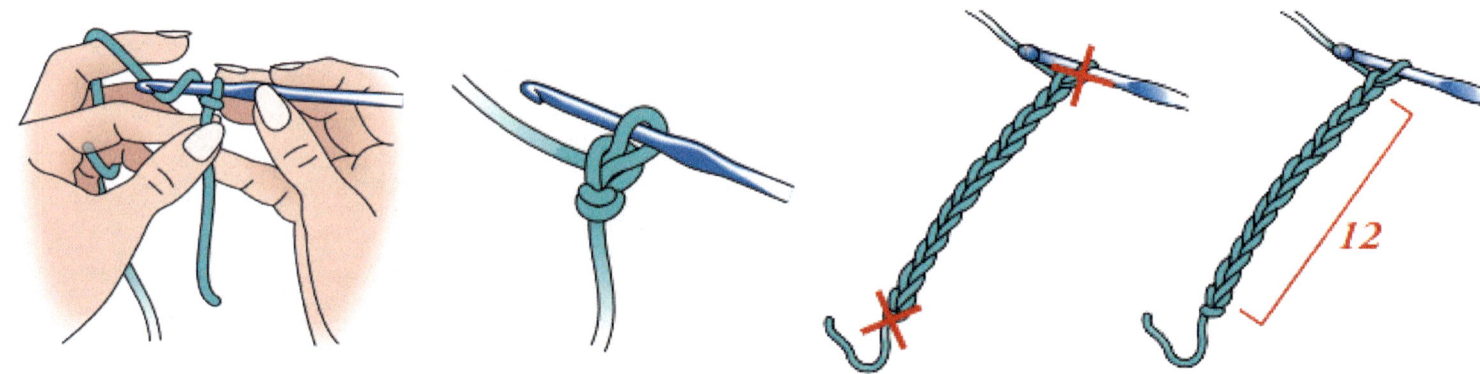

1. Yarn over and pull the yarn through the loop already on the hook to form a new loop. Be careful not to tighten the previous loop

2. Repeat Step 1 to form the number of chains specified in the instructions. Do not count the slip knot or the loop on the hook as a stitch.

Working Into the Foundation Chain

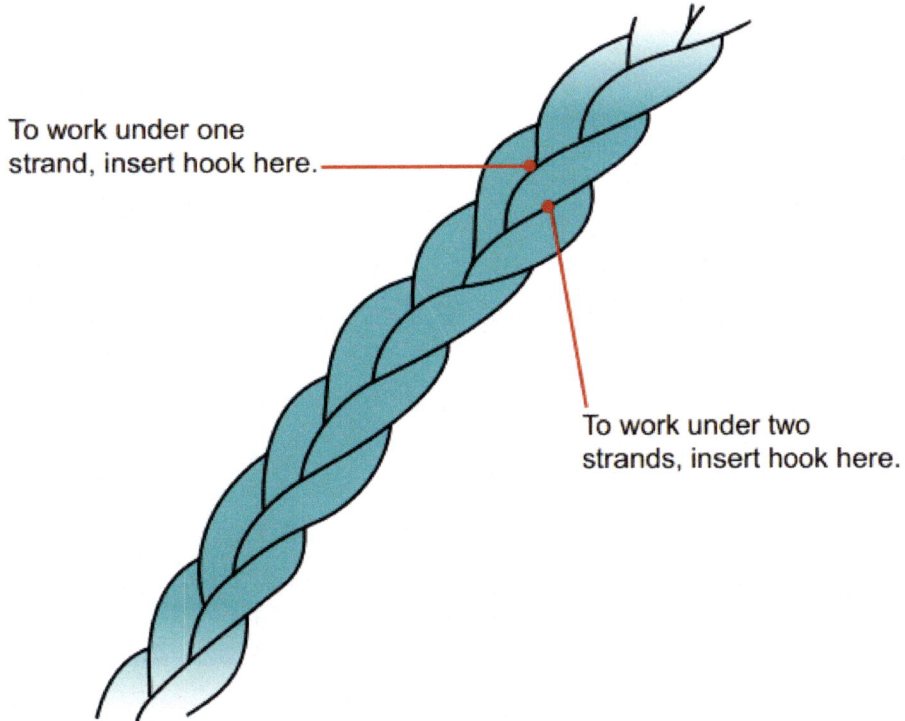

When working into the starting chain, you may work under one or two strands of chain loops as shown above. Either of these methods forms an even, firm bottom edge. Whether the basic stitches are worked into a starting chain or worked into previous rows, the method is the same.

You may like to work into the "bump" on the back of the chain. This forms an even, stretchy bottom edge that is ideal for garments.

Whichever method of working into the foundation you choose, be consistent. Work all pieces of a project in the same manner.

Basic Stitches

Whether the basic stitches are worked into a starting chain or worked into previous rows, the method is the same

Slip Stitch (sl st)

This is the shortest of all crochet stitches. Unlike other stitches, slip stitches are not usually used on their own to produce a fabric. The slip stitch is used for joining, shaping and, where necessary, to move the yarn to another part of the fabric for the next step.

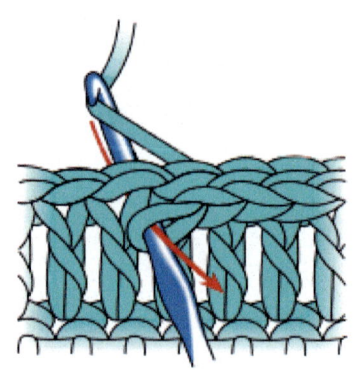

2. When working into previous rows, yarn over and pull the yarn through both the work and the loop on the hook in one movement

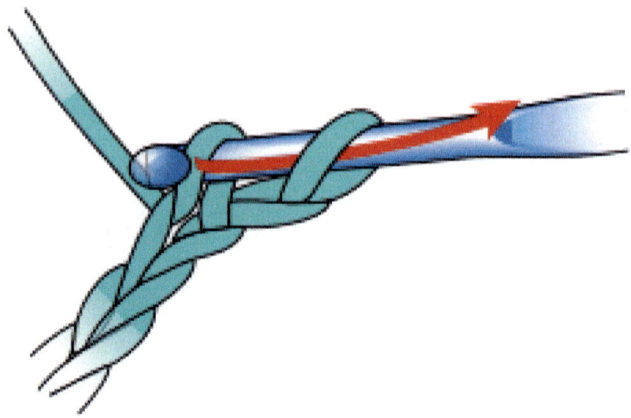

1. Insert the hook into the work as directed in pattern. Yarn over and pull the yarn through in one movement.

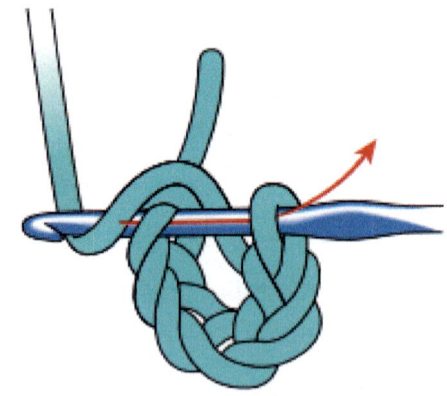

3. To join a chain ring with a slip stitch, insert the hook into first chain, yarn over and pull the yarn through the work and the loop on the hook

Single Crochet (sc) ✚

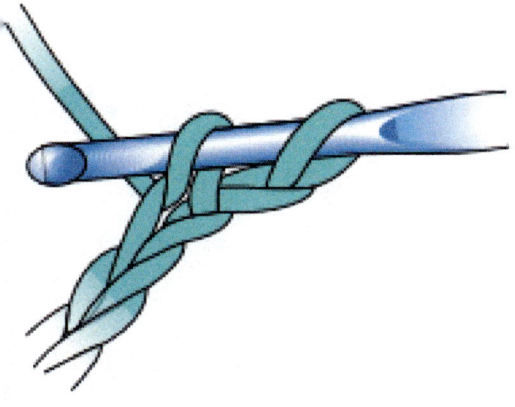
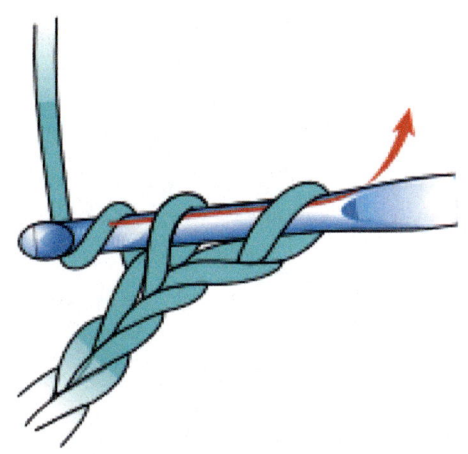
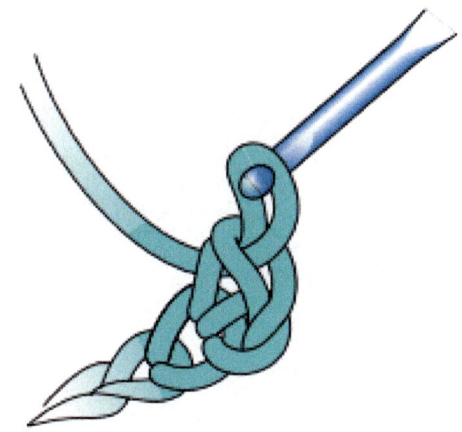

1. Insert the hook into the work (second chain from hook on the starting chain), * yarn over and pull up a loop

2. Yarn over again and pull the yarn through both loops on the hook

3. 1 sc made. Insert hook into next stitch; repeat from * in step 1

Half Double Crochet (hdc) T

1. Yarn over and insert the hook into the work (third chain from hook on the starting chain).

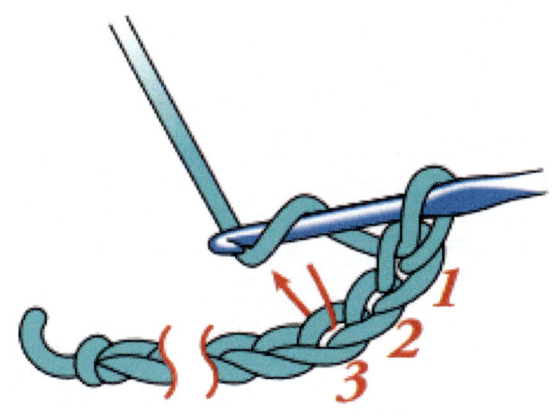

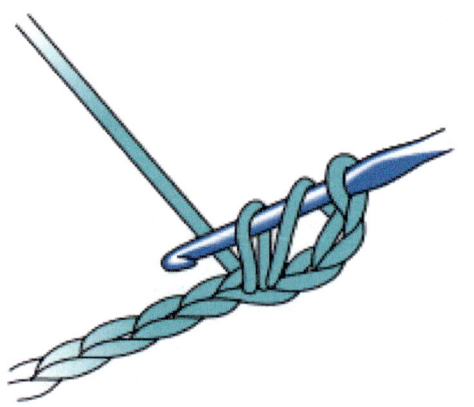 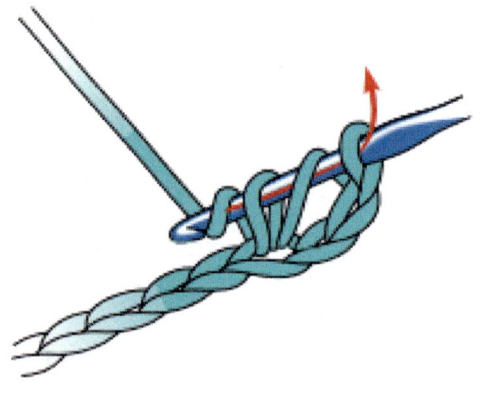 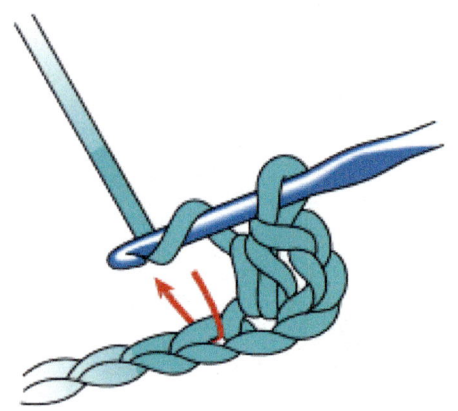

2. * Yarn over and draw through pulling up a loop.

3. Yarn over again and pull yarn through all three loops on the hook

4. 1 hdc made. Yarn over, insert hook into next stitch; repeat from * in step 2.

Double Crochet (dc)

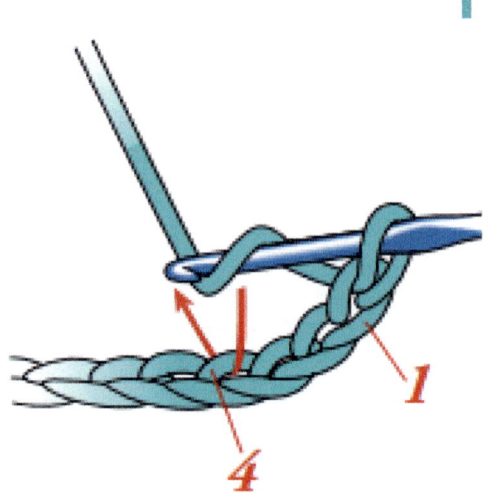 

1. Yarn over and insert the hook into the work (fourth chain from hook on starting chain)

2. * Yarn over and draw yarn through pulling up a loop.

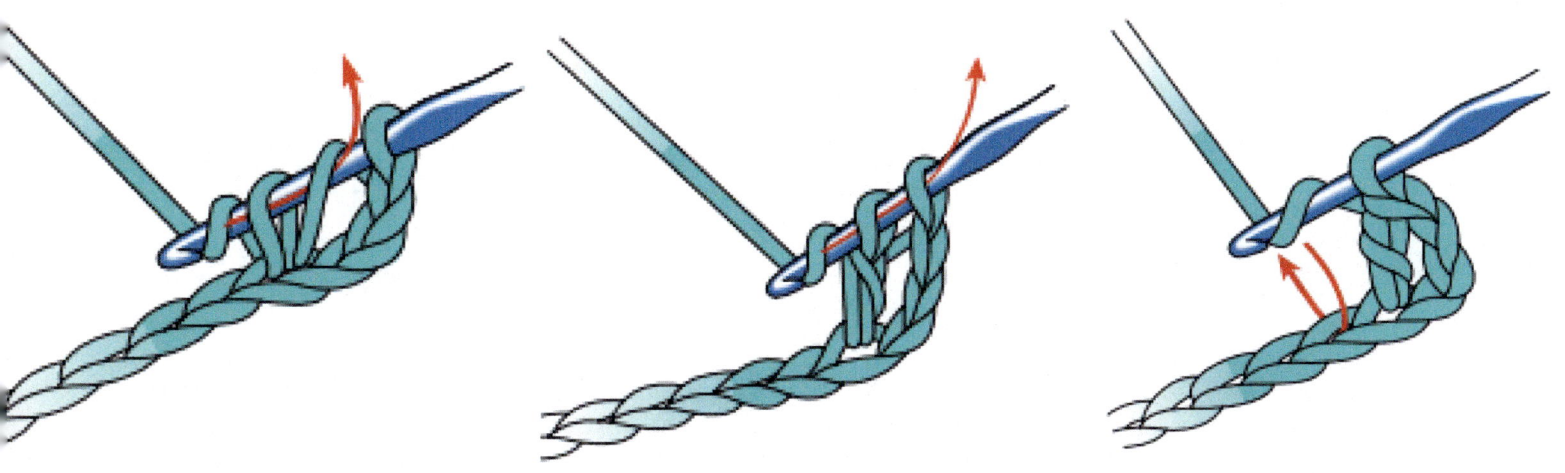

3. Yarn over and pull yarn through the first two loops only on the hook.

4. Yarn over and pull yarn through the last two loops on the hook.

5. 1 dc made. Yarn over, insert hook into next stitch; repeat from * in Step 2

Treble (tr)

1. Yarn over twice, insert the hook into the work (fifth chain from hook on the starting chain).

2. * Yarn over and draw yarn through pulling up a loop

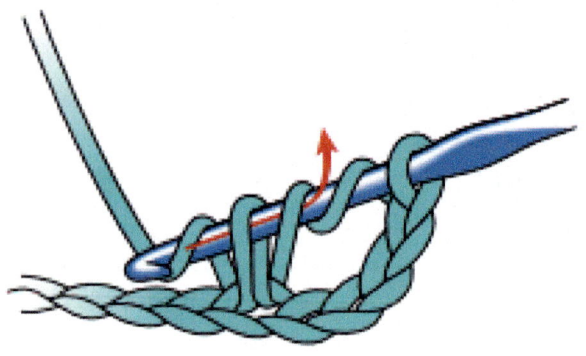

3. Yarn over again and pull yarn through the first two loops only on the hook

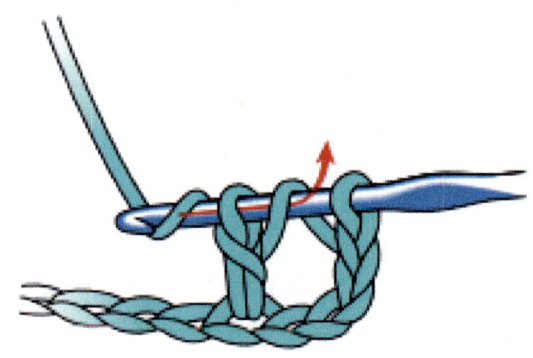

4. Yarn over again and pull yarn through the next two loops only on the hook.

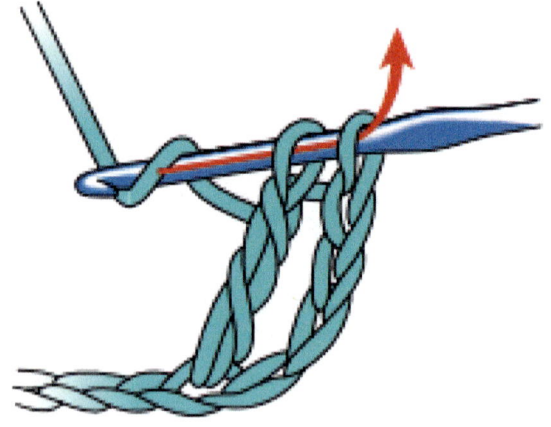

5. Yarn over again and pull yarn through the last two loops on the hook.

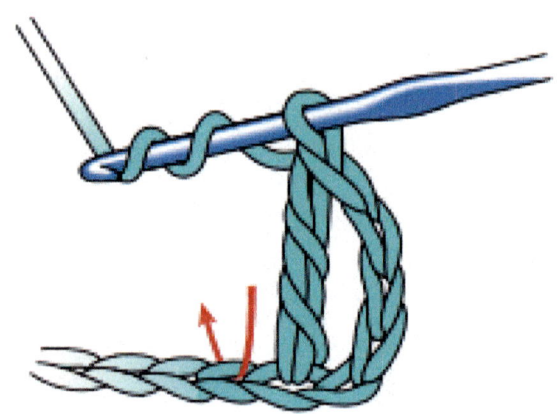

6. 1 tr made. Yarn over twice, insert hook into next stitch; repeat from * in Step 2.

Longer Basic Stitches:

Double treble (dtr), triple treble (ttr), quadruple treble (qtr) etc., are made by wrapping the yarn over three, four, five times, etc., at the beginning and finishing as for a treble crochet, repeating Step 4 until two loops remain on hook, and then finishing with Step 5.

Making Crochet Fabric

Starting Chain

To make a flat crocheted fabric worked in rows, you must begin with a starting chain. The length of the starting chain is the number of stitches needed for the first row of fabric plus the number of chains needed to get to the correct height of the first stitch used in the first row.

Turning Chains

When turning a row, the first chain (turning chain) helps transition the row to the height of the first stitch of the new row. The height of the first chain (turning chain) must match the height of the first stitch, and the number of chains depends on the first stitch after the chain

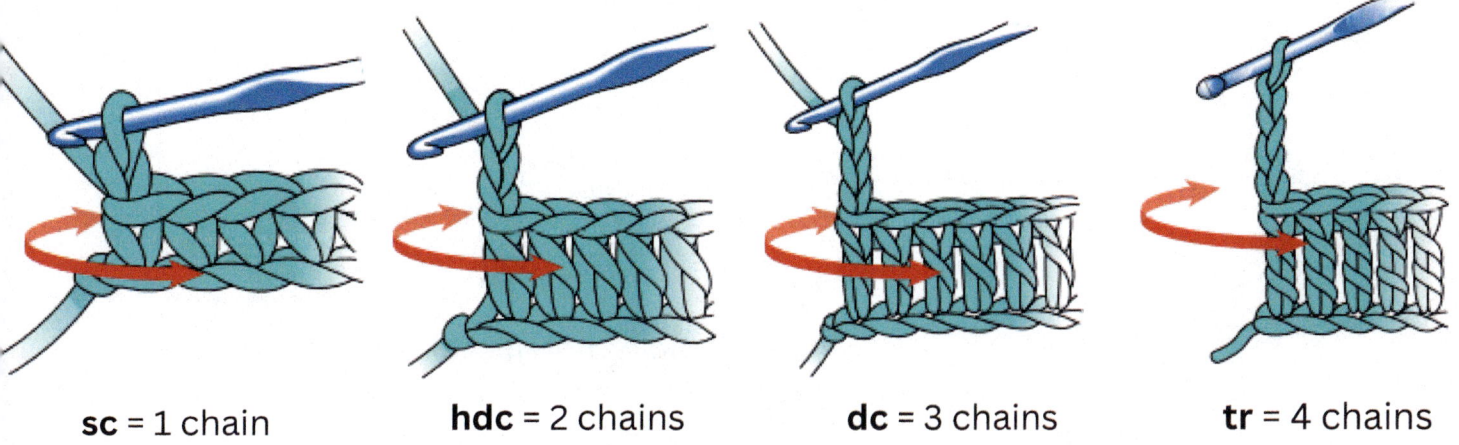

sc = 1 chain   hdc = 2 chains   dc = 3 chains   tr = 4 chains

When working half double crochet or other longer stitches, the turning chain usually the first stitch (the project instructions will let you know if the turning chains are not considered a stitch). When one chain is worked at the beginning of a row starting with a single crochet stitch, it is usually for height only and is made in addition to the first stitch.

Basic Double Crochet Fabric

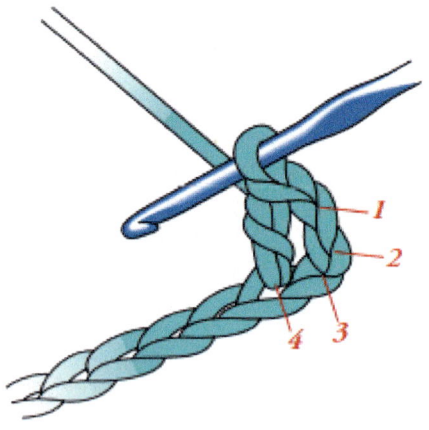

Make a starting chain of the required length plus two chains. Work one double crochet into fourth chain from hook. The three chains at the beginning of the row form the first double crochet.

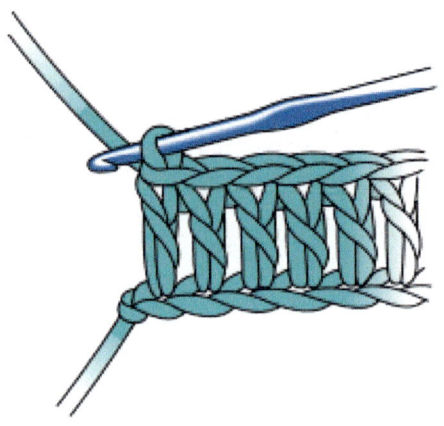

Work one double crochet into the next chain and every chain to the end of the row.

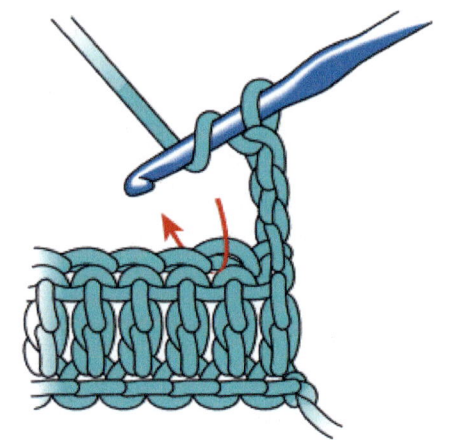

At the end of each crochet row, turn the work so that another row can be crocheted across the top of the previous row. It does not matter which way the work is turned but be consistent. Make three chains for turning (which are then counted as the first double crochet). Skip the first double crochet in the previous row, work a double crochet into the top of the next and every double crochet including last double crochet in row.

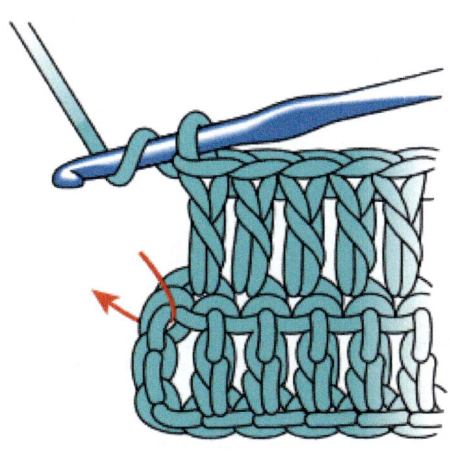

Work the last double crochet into third of three chains at the beginning of the previous row

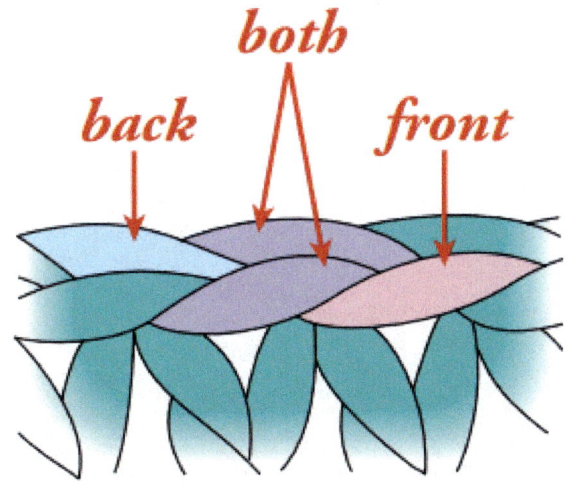

Note: The project instructions may specify if you are to work into the front or back loop of the stitch in the row below. Unless otherwise stated, always work under two strands of the top of the stitch in the row below

Increasing and Decreasing

To increase: 2 or more stitches are worked into 1 stitch at the point specified in the project instructions. Single crochet, half double crochet, double crochet and longer stitches are all increased in the same manner.

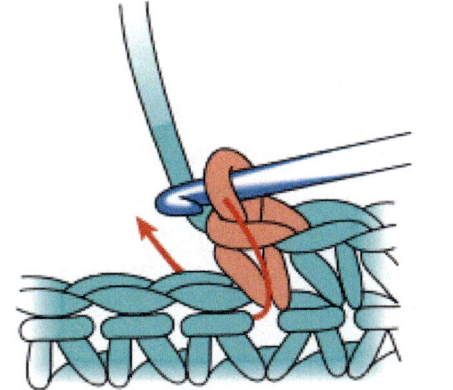  

To decrease: 2 or more stitches are worked together, by leaving the last loop of each stitch on the hook then working them off together. Single crochet, half double crochet, and longer stitches can be decreased in this way, called sc2tog, hdc2tog, etc.

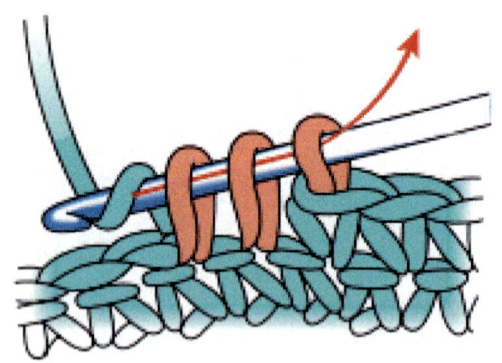

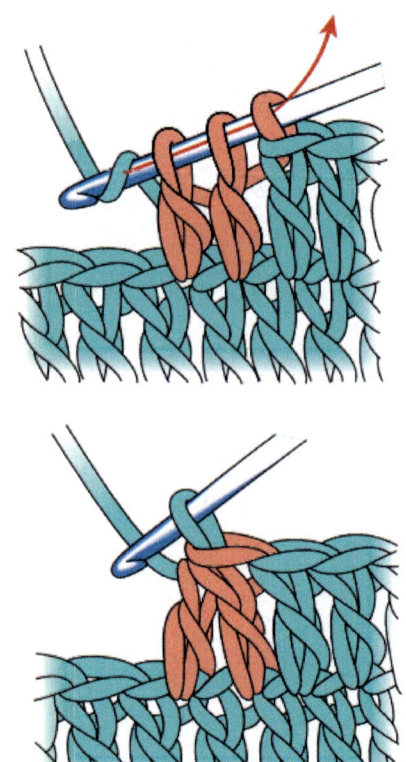

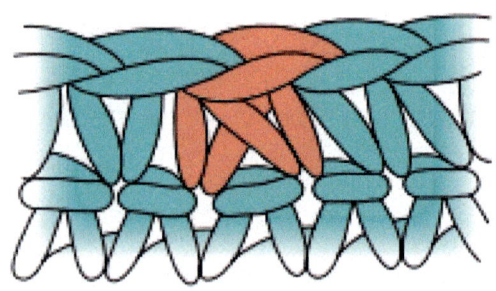

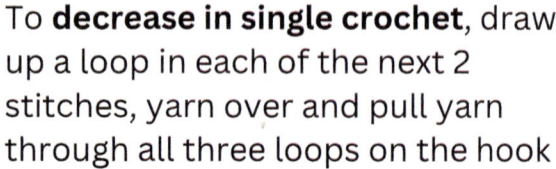

To **decrease in single crochet**, draw up a loop in each of the next 2 stitches, yarn over and pull yarn through all three loops on the hook

Many pattern stitches incorporate the increase and decrease method. See Shell Stitch and Cluster Stitch

To **decrease in double crochet**, yarn over and draw up a loop in the next stitch, yarn over and pull yarn through two loops only on the hook, yarn over and draw up a loop in the next stitch, yarn over and pull yarn through two loops only on the hook, yarn over and pull yarn through the remaining three loops on the hook.

Working in Rounds

Most motifs are not worked in rows but are worked in rounds from the center out. Unless otherwise stated in the pattern instructions, do not turn the work between rounds but continue with the same side facing and treat this as the right side of the fabric. The center ring is usually formed by a number of chains joined together with a slip stitch to form a ring.

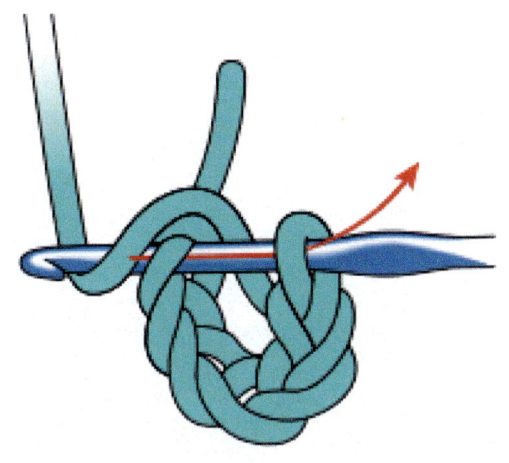

1. Insert the hook into the first chain made

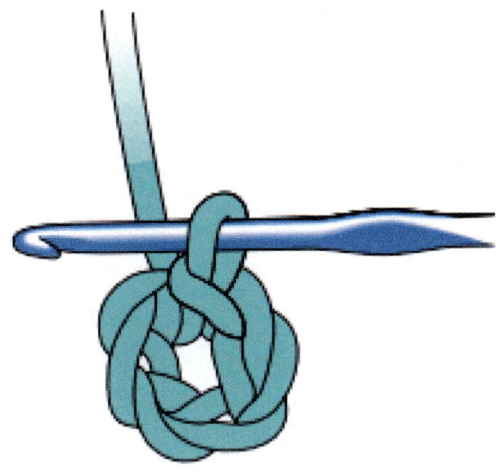

2. Make a slip stitch to join the chains into a ring.

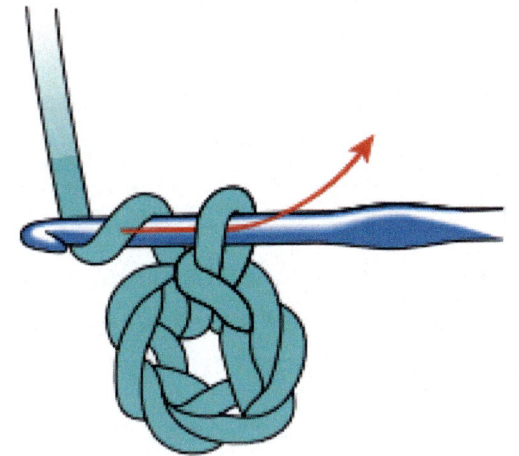

3. At the beginning of each round, one or more chain(s) can be worked to match the height of the following stitches. (This is equal to a turning chain.) When working in double crochet, three starting chains are required.

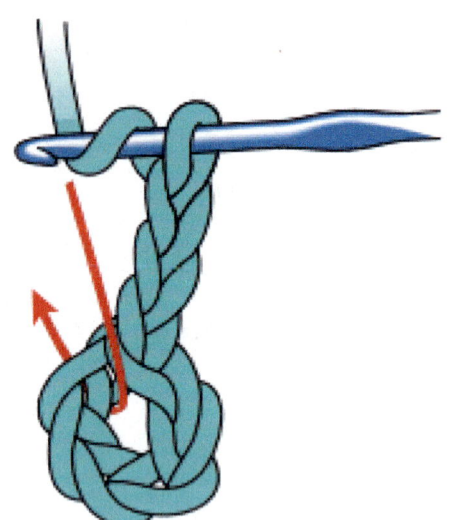

4. The stitches of the first round are worked by inserting the hook into the empty circle space at the center of the ring. Sometimes the first round is worked into the first chain—the pattern will specify how to form the first round.

5. When each round is complete, insert the hook into the top of the chain or stitch at the beginning of the round and make a slip stitch to close the round.

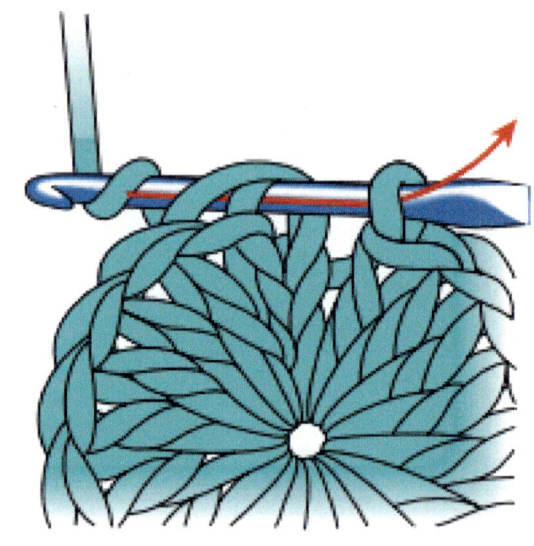

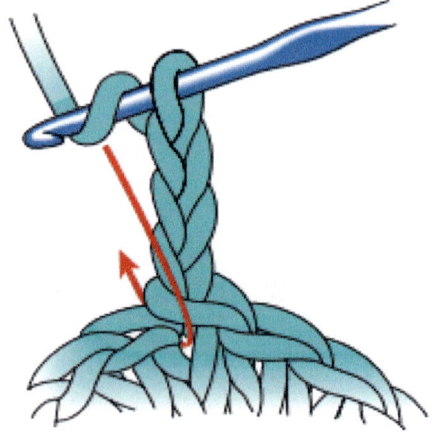

6. When working the second and subsequent rounds, unless otherwise stated, insert the hook under the two top loops of the stitches in the previous round.

After joining the final round with a slip stitch, fasten off by making one chain, then cutting the yarn and drawing the end through. Pull gently to tighten and form a knot.

Magic Ring

A magic ring is the ideal way to start crocheting in the round. You start by crocheting over an adjustable loop and finally pull the loop tight when you have finished the required number of stitches.

The advantage of this method is that there's no hole left in the middle of your starting round.

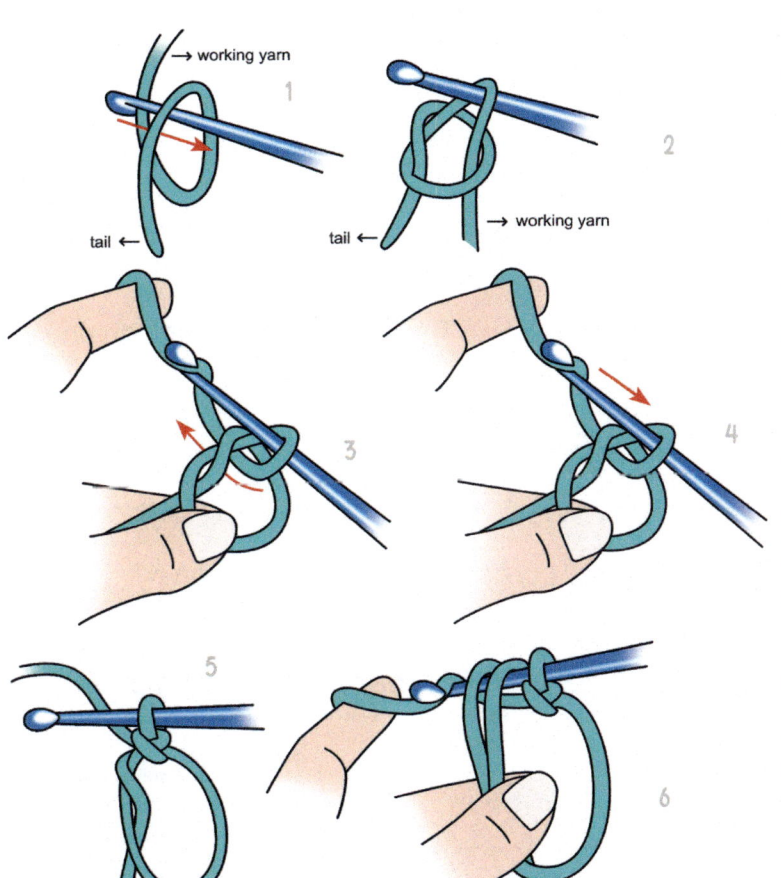

Start with the yarn crossed to form a circle (1).

Draw up a loop with your hook but don't pull it tight (2).

Hold the circle with your index finger and thumb and wrap the working yarn over your middle finger (3).

Make one chain stitch by wrapping the yarn over the hook and pulling it through
the loop on your hook (4, 5).

Now insert your hook into the loop and underneath the tail. Wrap the yarn over the hook and draw up a loop (6).

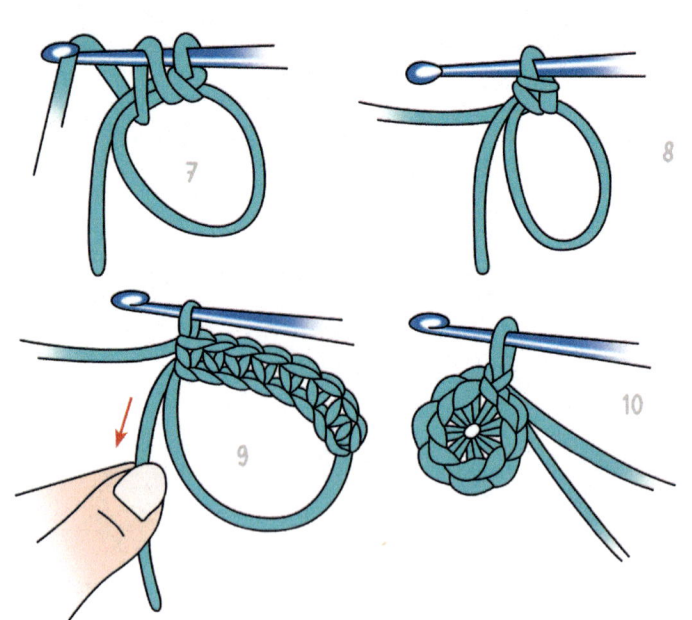

Wrap the yarn over the hook again (7) and draw it through both loops on your hook.

You have now completed your first single crochet stitch (8).

Continue to crochet (repeating step 6, 7, 8) until you have the required number of stitches as mentioned in the pattern.

Now grab the yarn tail and pull to draw the center of the ring tightly closed (9, 10).

You can now begin your second round by crocheting into the first single crochet stitch of the magic ring. You can use a stitch marker to remember where you started.

If you don't prefer this technique, you can start each piece using the following technique:
ch 2, x sc into the second chain from the hook – where x is the number of sc stitches you would make in your magic ring.

Stitch Variations

Most crochet stitch patterns, no matter how complex they seem, are made using combinations of basic stitches. Different effects can be created by small variations in the stitch making procedure or by varying the position and manner of inserting the hook into the fabric.

Note: Many patterns refer to certain groups of stitches in the instructions, but be careful—"bobble", "cluster", "shell", etc., may not mean the same thing from pattern to pattern. Always read the instructions carefully

Groups or Shells

Shells and groups consist of several complete stitches worked into the same place. They can be worked as part of a stitch pattern or as a method of increasing. Groups and shells can be worked in half double crochet, double crochet or longer stitches.

Five Double Crochet Shell

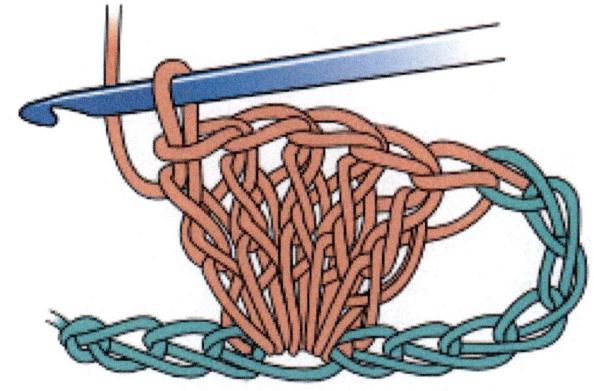

Work five double crochet stitches in one stitch.

Clusters

Any combination of stitches may be joined into a cluster by leaving the last loop of each stitch on the hook until they are worked off together at the end. Working stitches together in this way can also be a method of decreasing.

Be sure to read the instructions carefully to see how and where the hook should be inserted for each "leg" of the cluster. The "legs" can be worked over adjacent stitches, or stitches can be skipped in between the "legs".

Clusters can be worked in half double crochet, double crochet or longer stitches

Three Double Crochet Cluster

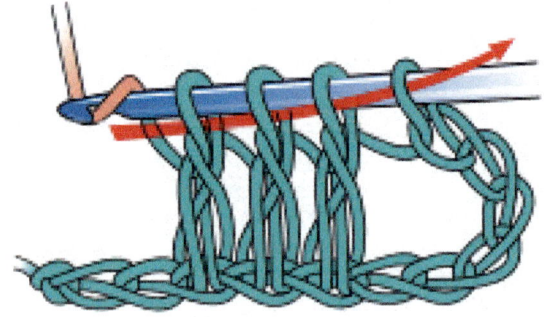

1. Work a double crochet into each of the next three stitches, holding the last loop of each double crochet on the hook

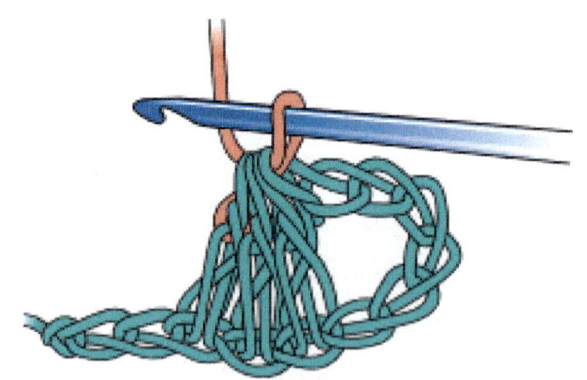

2. Yarn over and pull the yarn through all four loops on the hook

Bobbles

When a cluster is worked into one stitch, it forms a bobble. Bobbles can be worked in double crochet or longer stitches

Five Double Crochet Bobble

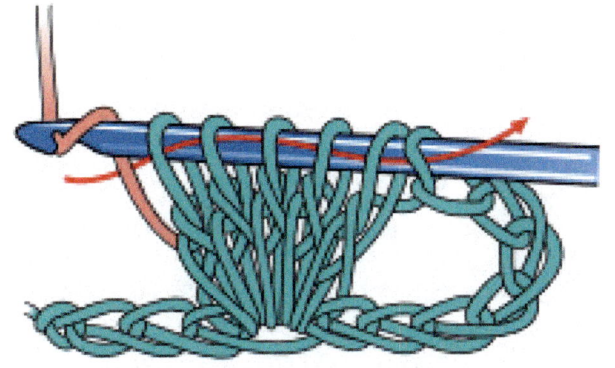

1. Work five double crochet into one stitch, leaving the last loop of each on the hook. Yarn over and pull yarn through all six loops on the hook.

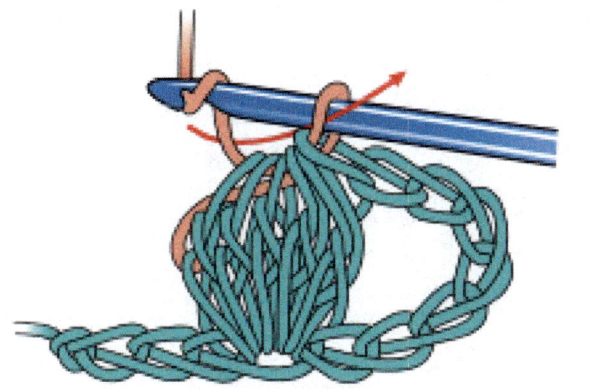

2. Bobbles made with more double crochet stitches or with heavy yarn can be closed and secured with an extra chain stitch.

Popcorns

Popcorns are groups of complete stitches usually worked into the same place, folded and closed at the top. They can be worked in half double crochet, double crochet or longer stitches. An extra chain can be worked to close and secure the top of the popcorn.

Five Double Crochet Popcorn

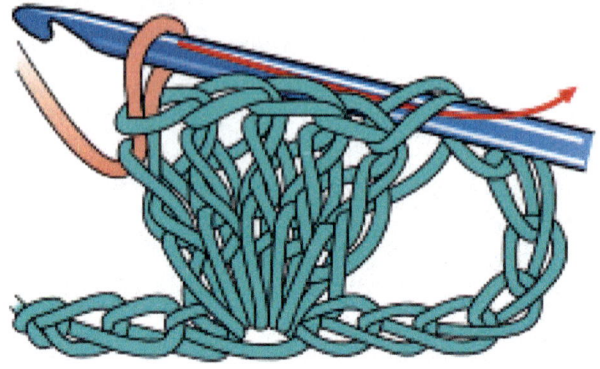

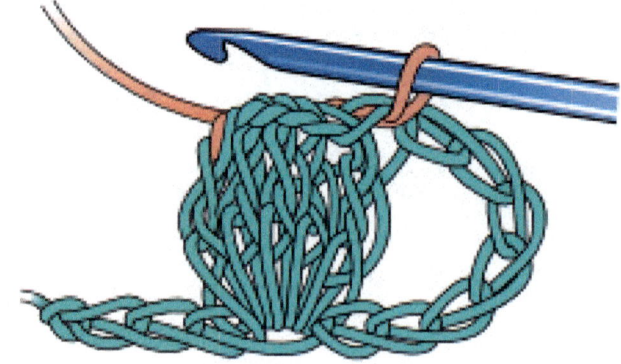

1. Work five double crochet into one stitch. Remove the hook from the working loop and insert it from front to back into the top of the first double crochet in the group

2. Pick up the working loop on the last stitch made and pull this loop through the first stitch to close the popcorn. If the instructions specify it, work one chain to close and secure the popcorn.

Puff Stitches

These are similar to bobbles but are worked, using half double crochet, into the same stitch or space. However, because of the way a half double crochet stitch is constructed, it cannot be worked until one loop remains on the hook. The puff stitch is not closed until the required number of stitches have been worked.

Three Half Double Crochet Puff Stitch

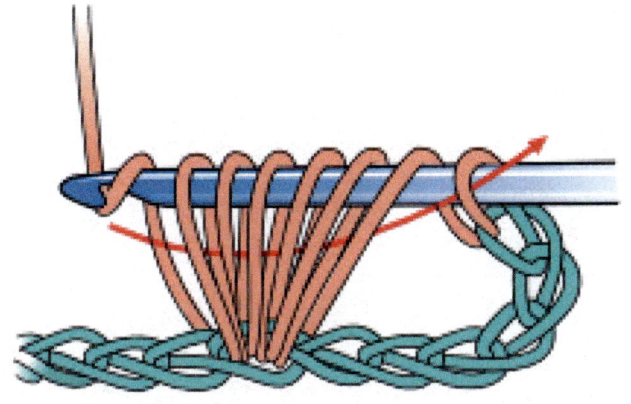
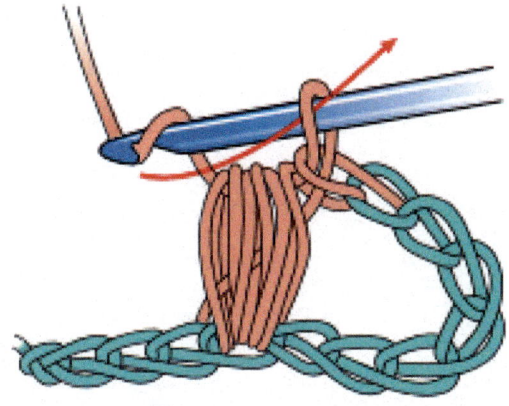

1. Yarn over, insert the hook in specified stitch, yarn over again and draw a loop through (three loops on hook). Repeat two more times, inserting the hook into the same stitch (seven loops on the hook); yarn over and pull yarn through all seven loops on the hook.

2. As with popcorns and bulky bobbles, an extra chain stitch is often used to secure the puff stitch firmly. The pattern will tell you if this is necessary.

Fastening Off

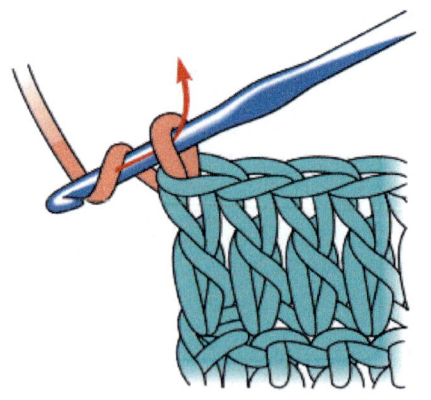

To fasten off the yarn permanently, cut the yarn leaving an 8" end (longer if you need to sew pieces together). Pull the end of the yarn through the loop on the hook and pull gently to tighten

Joining in New Yarn and Changing Colors

When joining in new yarn or changing color, continue in the working yarn until two loops of the last stitch remain in the working yarn or color.

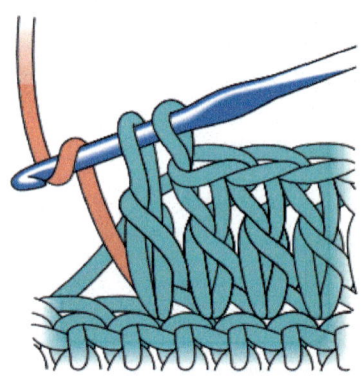
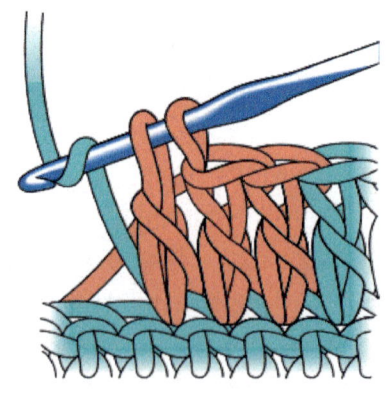

Yarn over with the new color of yarn and pull the new color of yarn through to complete the stitch.

Continue to work the following stitches in the new color of yarn following the pattern instructions.

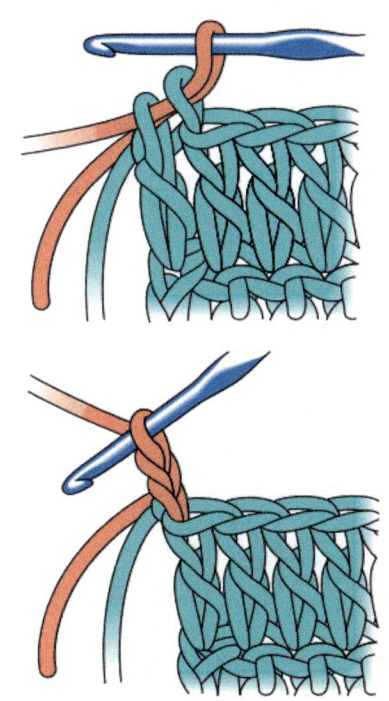

If you are working whole rows in different colors, make the change during the last stitch in the previous row, so the new color for the next row is ready to work the turning chain

If you are working a narrow stripe pattern, instead of cutting off the old color or yarn, carry it loosely along the side of the fabric so that it is ready to pick up again the next time it is needed. For wide stripe patterns, it is usually best to cut off the old color or yarn, leaving a 6" end for weaving in. Longer carries, or "floats", are easily snagged

Reading a Crochet Pattern

In order to follow crochet instructions, you should know how to make the basic stitches and be familiar with basic fabric-making procedures. You should also be familiar with the abbreviations for the basic stitches.

Gauge

Gauge refers to the number of stitches and rows in a given area. When following a pattern for a garment or other project, the instructions will include a specified gauge. If you do not crochet fabric with the same number of stitches and rows as indicated, your pieces will not be the measurements given. To ensure that you achieve the correct gauge, work a sample or swatch before starting to crochet the actual project. The hook size stated in the pattern is a suggested hook size only. Use whichever hook gives you the correct gauge.

Finishing

Finishing methods for crochet depend largely on the end purpose of the crochet (afghan, pillow, garment) and the yarn you use to create the piece.

Weaving in Ends

Weave in ends securely before blocking pieces or sewing seams. Securely woven ends will not come loose with wear or washing. It's best to work in ends as invisibly as possible.

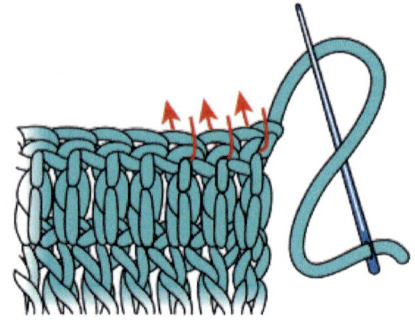

1. Thread yarn end through a blunt tapestry needle. Whipstitch the end around several stitches. Trim the end close to work.

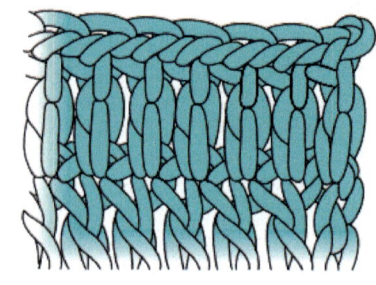

2. The woven end should be nearly invisible.

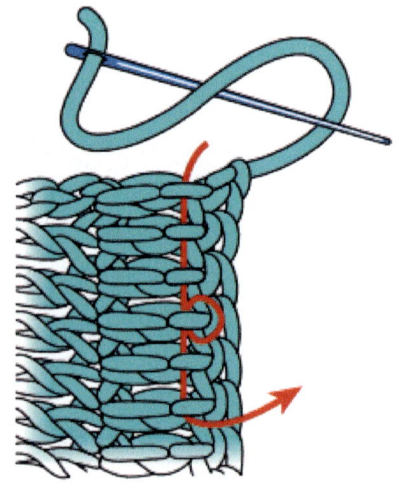

3. Another method of weaving in ends is to run the end under several stitches, wrap it around a stitch and then run it under several more stitches. For even more security, reverse the direction and weave back under and over a few more stitches. Trim the end close to work

Joining Seams

Various methods can be used to join pieces of crochet and, again, the use of the finished item often dictates the assembly method. Sewn seams can be invisible or decorative. Below are a few suggestions for joining pieces of crochet.

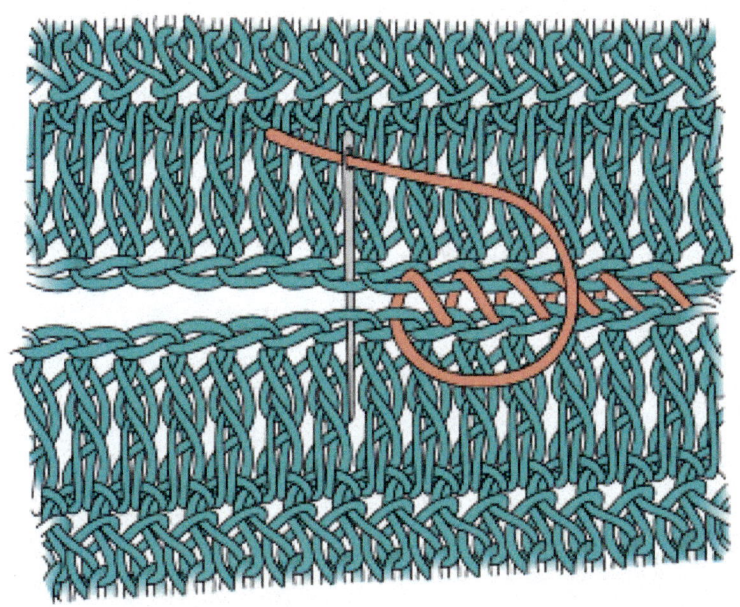

To join with an invisible sewn seam, place pieces edge to edge with the wrong sides facing up and whipstitch together.

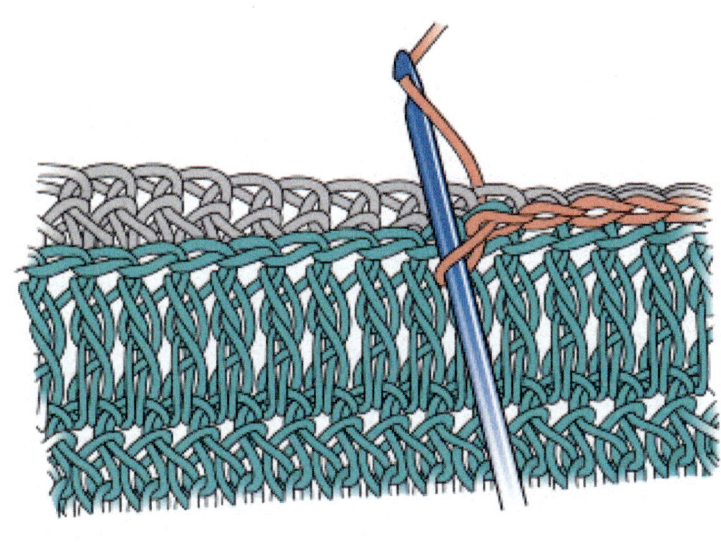

To join invisibly using a crochet hook, place right sides of pieces together and slip stitch through one loop of each piece as illustrated.

Blocking and Pressing

Acrylic and acrylic blends: Blocking items made with acrylic yarn is not usually necessary. If you feel blocking will help make the garment look better, block as for cotton items, but do not press, just let the pieces dry thoroughly before removing any pins.

Cotton: Lay the crocheted pieces wrong side up on a flat padded surface (such as the top of an ironing board or a mattress protected with a layer of clean towels), gently stretching and shaping to the measurements specified. Pin in place with rustproof pins. Dampen the piece. If starching is required (for a crocheted doily, for instance) dab the starch onto the piece using a clean cloth or a soft, clean paintbrush. Then press using a hot iron. Do not allow the full weight of the iron to rest on the work, especially if the piece contains highly textured stitches such as bobbles and popcorns. Remove the pins and, if necessary, make small adjustments to the edges of the piece to ensure that they are straight. Repin and let pieces dry thoroughly before moving them.

Abbreviation

Abbreviation	Description
BLO	back loop only
bo	bobble
BP	back post
BPdc	back post double crochet
BPdtr	back post double treble crochet
BPhdc	back post half double crochet
BPsc	back post single crochet
BPtr	back post treble crochet
ch	chain stitch
ch-sp	chain space
CL	cluster
dc	double crochet
dc2tog	double crochet 2 stitches together
dec	decrease
dtr	double treble crochet
FLO	front loop only
FP	front post
FPdc	front post double crochet
FPdtr	front post double treble crochet
FPhdc	front post half double crochet
FPsc	front post single crochet
FPtr	front post treble crochet

Abbreviation	Description
hdc	half double crochet
hdc2tog	half double crochet 2 stitches together
inc	increase
pm	place marker
puff	puff stitch
rem	remaining
rep	repeat
rnd	round
RS	right side
sc	single crochet
sc2tog	single crochet 2 stitches together
sh	shell
sl st	slip stitch
sp	space
st	stitch
tog	together
tr	treble crochet
WS	wrong side
yo	yarn over
yoh	yarn over hook

Term	Description
*	repeat the instructions following the single asterisk a directed
* *	repeat instructions between asterisks as many times as directed or repeat at specified locations
[ ]	number of stitches at the end of each round/row
( )	work instructions within parentheses as many times as directed or work a group of stitches all in the same stitch or space

Measurement	Description
" or in	inch
cm	centimeter
g	gram
m	meter
mm	millimeter
oz	ounce
yd	yard

Abbreviation & Term Differences between the U.S., United Kingdom (U.K.) and Canada.

U.S./Canada	**U.K.**
slip stitch (sl st)	slip stitch (ss)
single crochet (sc)	double crochet (dc)
half double crochet (hdc)	half treble (htr)
double crochet (dc)	treble (tr)
treble (tr)	double treble (dtr)
double treble (dtr)	triple treble (trtr)

U.S.U.K./Canada	**U.K./Canada**
gauge	tension
yarn over (yo)	yarn over hook (yoh)

CHAPTER II.

Crochet Dog Sweaters Patterns

Materials:

- Brava Worsted Weight Yarn
  - approx. 110 yards for XS
  - approx. 205 yards for S
  - approx. 375 yards for M
- Crochet hook in size H/5mm
- **Gauge: 14 sts x 13 rows = 4"**

Size	Neck (up to)	Chest (up to)
XS	8"	14"
S	12"	18"
M	15"	24"

Pattern notes:

- Pattern written using US terms.
- The chain at the beginning of the row does not count as a stitch.
- Front post/Back post stitches are used for the collar.
- The body of this sweater uses the Thicket (aka Suzette) stitch.

Special Stiches:

- Lsc = Insert hook in indicated stitch 2 rows below and draw up a loop. Yoh and draw through 2 loops on hook. Skip st behind Lsc.
- Sc2tog = Draw up a loop in each of next 2 sc. Yoh and draw through all 3 loops on hook
- Scbl = Single crochet in back loop only

Instructions

Gauge pattern:

Row 1: Ch-18. (sc, dc) in 2nd ch from hook. * sk next ch, (sc, dc) in next * repeat between * * 6 more times. Sk next ch, sc in last. (17)

Rows 2 – 14: Ch-1, turn, * (sc, dc) in next st, sk next st * repeat between * * 7 more times. Sk next st, sc in last. (17) Measure for gauge.

Note on gauge: Always make your swatch slightly larger than it needs to be so that when you measure you are only including inside stitches, not the outside stitches that are not uniform in shape.

Collar:

Row 1: Fhdc– (33, 43, 53) (or ch- (34, 44, 54), hdc in 2nd chain from hook and in each to end.) Join to top of first st with sl st. Stitch count: (33, 43, 53)

Row 2: Ch-1, do not turn, * fphdc around next st, bphdc around next st * repeat between * * around, fphdc around last st. Join to top of first fphdc with sl st. Stitch count: (33, 43, 53)

Row 3: Ch-1, turn, * bphdc around next st, fphdc around next st * repeat between * * around, bphdc around last st. Join to top of first bphdc with sl st. Stitch count: (33, 43, 53)

Row 4: Ch-1, turn, * fphdc around next st, bphdc around next st * repeat between * * around, fphdc around last st. Join to top of first fphdc with sl st. Stitch count: (33, 43, 53)

Rows 5 through (6, 8, 10): alternate rows 3 & 4. Stitch count: (33, 43, 53)

Chest/Body:

Row (7, 9, 11): Ch-1, do not turn. (sc, dc) in first st. * sk next st, (sc, dc) in next * repeat between * * around, sk next, (sc, dc, sc) in last st. Join to top of first sc with sl st. Stitch count: (35, 45, 55)

Row (8, 10, 12): Ch-1, turn, (sc, dc) in first st. * sk next st, (sc, dc) in next * repeat between * * around, sk next, (sc, dc, sc) in last st. Join to top of first sc with sl st. Stitch count: (37, 47, 57)

Rows (9, 11, 13) through (13, 17, 25): repeat previous row. Stitch count: (47, 61, 83)

Row (14, 18, 26): Ch-1, turn, (sc, dc) in first st. * sk next st, (sc, dc) in next * repeat between * * around (do not do the extra sc). Join to top of first sc with sl st. Stitch count: (48, 62, 84)

Armholes:

Row (15, 19, 27): Ch-1, turn * sk next st, (sc, dc) in next * repeat between * * (0,1, 2) more times. (2, 4, 6 sts total so far). Sk next st, sc in next. Ch-(7, 11, 15), sk-(9, 13, 17) sts. In next sc, place (sc, dc). Repeat between * * (10, 11, 17) more times. Sk next st, sc in next. Ch-(7, 11, 15), sk-(9, 13, 17) sts. In next sc, place (sc, dc). Repeat between * * to end. Join to top of first sc with sl st. Stitch count: (44, 58, 80)

Row (16, 20, 28): Ch-1, turn. * Sk next st, (sc, dc) in next * repeat between * * around (including chains). Join to top of first sc with sl st. Stitch count: (44, 58, 80)

Rows (17, 21, 29) through (20, 30, 44): Ch-1, turn, * sk next st, (sc, dc) in next * repeat between * * around. Join to top of first sc with sl st. Stitch count: (44, 58, 80)

Begin body tapering:

Row (21, 31, 45): Ch-1, turn, sl st in first (2, 4, 6,) sts, * sk next st, (sc, dc) in next * repeat between * * (18, 23, 32) more times. Sk next st, sc in next. (Leave remaining 2, 4, 6) sts unworked) Stitch count: (39, 49, 67) not including sl sts.

Row (22, 32, 46): Ch-1, turn, sk first 2 sts, * (sc, dc) in next, sk next st * repeat between * * (17, 22, 31) more times. Sc in next st. Stitch count: (37, 47, 65)

Row (23, 33, 47): Ch-1, turn, sk first 2 sts, * (sc, dc) in next, sk next st * repeat between * * (16, 21, 30) more times. Sc in next st. Stitch count: (35, 45, 63)

Continue decreasing until you reach row (36, 46, 66) ending with (9, 19, 25) sts.

Row (37, 47, 67): Ch-1, turn, sc in each st/row end around

Materials:

- Brava Worsted Weight Yarn
-approx. 550 yards for L
-approx. 650 yards for XL
-approx. 750 yards for XXL
- Crochet hook in size H/5mm
- (6) 1" (or 1.25") Buttons
- **Gauge: 14 sts x 13 rows = 4"**

Size	Neck (up to)	Chest (up to)
L	16"	30"
XL	18"	33"
XXL	20"	36"

Pattern notes:

- Pattern written using US terms.
- The chain at the beginning of the row does not count as a stitch.
- Front post/Back post stitches are used for the collar.
- The body of this sweater uses the Thicket (aka Suzette) stitch.
- Odd numbered rows are "right side".

Special Stiches:

- Lsc = Insert hook in indicated stitch 2 rows below and draw up a loop. Yoh and draw through 2 loops on hook. Skip st behind Lsc.
- Sc2tog = Draw up a loop in each of next 2 sc. Yoh and draw through all 3 loops on hook
- Scbl = Single crochet in back loop only

Instructions

Gauge pattern:

Row 1: Ch-18. (sc, dc) in 2nd ch from hook. * sk next ch, (sc, dc) in next * repeat between * * 6 more times. Sk next ch, sc in last. (17)

Rows 2 – 14: Ch-1, turn, * (sc, dc) in next st, sk next st * repeat between * * 7 more times. Sk next st, sc in last. (17) Measure for gauge.

Note: Always make your swatch slightly larger than it needs to be so that when you measure you are only including inside stitches, not the outside stitches that are not uniform in shape.

Collar:

Round 1: Fhdc– (63, 73, 83) (or ch- (64, 74, 84), hdc in 2nd chain from hook and in each to end.) Join to top of first st with sl st. Stitch count: (63, 73, 83)

Round 2: Ch-1, do not turn, * fphdc around next st, bphdc around next st * repeat between * * around, fphdc around last st. Join to top of first fphdc with sl st. Stitch count: (63, 73, 83)

Round 3: Ch-1, turn, * bphdc around next st, fphdc around next st * repeat between * * around, bphdc around last st. Join to top of first bphdc with sl st. Stitch count: (63, 73, 83)

Round 4: Ch-1, turn, * fphdc around next st, bphdc around next st * repeat between * * around, fphdc around last st. Join to top of first fphdc with sl st. Stitch count: (63, 73, 83)

Rounds 5 through 10: alternate rounds 3 & 4. Stitch count: (63, 73, 83)

Chest/Body:

Round 11: Ch-1, do not turn. (sc, dc) in first st. * sk next st, (sc, dc) in next * repeat between * * around. Join to top of first sc with sl st. Stitch count: (64, 74, 84)

Round 12: Ch-1, turn, * sk next st, (sc, dc) in next * repeat between * * (7, 8, 10) more times. (16, 18, 22 sts so far). Sc in next st. In next st place (hdc, sc). Sc in next st. In next st place (sc, dc). (22, 24, 28 sts so far). * sk next st, (sc, dc) in next * Repeat between * * around. Join to top of first sc with sl st. Stitch count: (66, 76, 86)

Round 13: repeat round 12. Stitch count: (68, 78, 88)

Round 14: Ch-1, turn, * sk next st, (sc, dc) in next * repeat between * * (16, 18, 21) more times, sc in next st, (hdc, sc) in next st, sc in next, (sc, dc) in next. Repeat between * * around. Join to top of first sc with sl st. Stitch count: (70, 80, 90)

Round 15: Ch-1, turn, * sk next st, (sc, dc) in next * repeat between * * around until you have 4 sts remaining. Sc in next st, (hdc, sc) in next st, sc in next, (sc, dc) in last st. Join to top of first sc with sl st. Stitch count: (72, 82, 92)

Round 16: Ch-1, turn, * sk next st, (sc, dc) in next * repeat between * * (8, 9, 11) more times, sc in next st, (hdc, sc) in next st, sc in next, (sc, dc) in next. Repeat between * * around. Join to top of first sc with sl st. Stitch count: (74, 84, 94)

Round 17: repeat round 16. Stitch count: (76, 86, 96)

Round 18: Ch-1, turn, * sk next st, (sc, dc) in next * repeat between * * (18, 20, 23) more times, sc in next st, (hdc, sc) in next st, sc in next, (sc, dc) in next. Repeat between * * around. Join to top of first sc with sl st. Stitch count: (78, 88, 98)

Round 19: repeat round 15. Stitch count: (80, 90, 100)

Round 20: Ch-1, turn, * sk next st, (sc, dc) in next * repeat between * * (9, 10, 12) more times, sc in next st, (hdc, sc) in next st, sc in next, (sc, dc) in next. Repeat between * * around. Join to top of first sc with sl st. Stitch count: (82, 92, 102)

Round 21: repeat round 20. Stitch count: (84, 94, 104)

Round 22: Ch-1, turn, * sk next st, (sc, dc) in next * repeat between * * (20, 22, 25) more times, sc in next st, (hdc, sc) in next st, sc in next, (sc, dc) in next. Repeat between * * around. Join to top of first sc with sl st. Stitch count: (86, 96, 106)

Round 23: Ch-1, turn, * sk next st, (sc, dc) in next * repeat between * * around until you have 4 sts remaining. Sc in next st, (hdc, sc) in next st, sc in next, (sc, dc) in last st. Join to top of first sc with sl st. Stitch count: (88, 98, 108)

Round 24: Ch-1, turn, * sk next st, (sc, dc) in next * repeat between * * (10, 11, 13) more times, sc in next st, (hdc, sc) in next st, sc in next, (sc, dc) in next. Repeat between * * around. Join to top of first sc with sl st. Stitch count: (90, 100, 110)

Round 25: repeat round 24. Stitch count: (92, 102, 112)

Round 26: Ch-1, turn, * sk next st, (sc, dc) in next * repeat between * * (22, 24, 27) more times, sc in next st, (hdc, sc) in next st, sc in next, (sc, dc) in next. Repeat between * * around. Join to top of first sc with sl st. Stitch count: (94, 104, 114)

Round 27: Ch-1, turn, * sk next st, (sc, dc) in next * repeat between * * around until you have 4 sts remaining. Sc in next st, (hdc, sc) in next st, sc in next, (sc, dc) in last st. Join to top of first sc with sl st. Stitch count: (96, 106, 116)

Round 28: Ch-1, turn, * sk next st, (sc, dc) in next * repeat between * * (11, 12, 15) more times, sc in next st, (hdc, sc) in next st, sc in next, (sc, dc) in next. Repeat between * * around. Join to top of first sc with sl st. Stitch count: (98, 108, 118)

Round 29: repeat row 28. Stitch count: (100, 110, 120)

Round/s (30, 30 – 32, 30 – 34): Ch-1, turn, * sk next st, (sc, dc) in next * repeat between * * around. Join to top of first sc with sl st. Stitch count: (100, 110, 120)

Place a stitch marker in the last stitch made. (Makes it easier to count below) Fasten off and weave in all ends.

Chest flap:

Looking at the "right" side (see pattern notes), attach yarn in (9th, 11th, 11th) stitch to the right of the chest seam. (should be a sc)

Row 1: Ch-1, (sc, dc) in same st. * sk next st, (sc, dc) in next * repeat between * * (7, 8, 9) more times. Stitch count: (18, 20, 22)

Rows 2 – (23, 25, 27): Ch-1, turn, * sk next st, (sc, dc) in next * repeat between * * to end. Stitch count: (18, 20, 22)

Fasten off and weave in all ends.

Back flap:

Looking at the "right" side, mark the (14th, 16th, 18th) stitch to the left of the chest flap. (Should be a sc)

Row 1: Ch-(16, 18, 20), (sc, dc) in marked stitch, *sk next st, (sc, dc) in next * repeat between * * (27, 29, 31) more times, ch-(16, 18, 20). Stitch count: (90, 98, 106)

Row 2: (sc, dc) in 2nd ch from hook. *sk next st, (sc, dc) in next * repeat between * * to end. Stitch count: (90, 98, 106)

Row 3: Ch-1, turn. * sk next st, (sc, dc) in next * repeat between * * to end. Stitch count: (90, 98, 106)

Row 4: (buttonhole row) Ch-1, turn, sk first st, (sc, dc) in next. Sk-3 sts, (sc, dc) in next. * sk next st, (sc, dc) in next * repeat between * * (39, 43, 47) more times. Sk-3 sts, (sc, dc) in last. Stitch count: (86, 94, 102)

Row 5: Ch-1, turn. Sk first 2 sts, (sc, dc, sc, dc) in hole. * sk next st, (sc, dc) in next * repeat between * * (39, 43, 47) times. (sc, dc, sc, dc) in hole, sk next st, (sc, dc) in last. Stitch count: (90, 98, 106)

Rows 6 – 8: Ch-1, turn. * sk next st, (sc, dc) in next * repeat between * * to end. Stitch count: (90, 98, 106)

Row 9: (buttonhole row) Ch-1, turn, sk first st, (sc, dc) in next. Sk-3 sts, (sc, dc) in next. * sk next st, (sc, dc) in next * repeat between * * (39, 43, 47) more times. Sk-3 sts, (sc, dc) in last. Stitch count: (86, 94, 102)

Row 10: Ch-1, turn. Sk first 2 sts, (sc, dc, sc, dc) in hole. * sk next st, (sc, dc) in next * repeat between * * (39, 43, 47) times. (sc, dc, sc, dc) in hole, sk next st, (sc, dc) in last. Stitch count: (90, 98, 106)

Rows 11 – 13: Ch-1, turn. * sk next st, (sc, dc) in next * repeat between * * to end. Stitch count: (90, 98, 106)

Row 14: (buttonhole row) Ch-1, turn, sk first st, (sc, dc) in next. Sk-3 sts, (sc, dc) in next. * sk next st, (sc, dc) in next * repeat between * * (39, 43, 47) more times. Sk-3 sts, (sc, dc) in last. Stitch count: (86, 94, 102)

Row 15: Ch-1, turn. Sk first 2 sts, (sc, dc, sc, dc) in hole. * sk next st, (sc, dc) in next * repeat between * * (39, 43, 47) times. (sc, dc, sc, dc) in hole, sk next st, (sc, dc) in last. Stitch count: (90, 98, 106)

Row 16: Ch-1, turn, sk first st, * (sc, dc) in next, sk next st * repeat between * * (43, 47, 51) more times. Sc in last st. Stitch count: (89, 97, 105)

Row 17: Ch-1, turn, sk first 2 sts, * (sc, dc) in next, sk next st * repeat between * * (42, 46, 50) more times. Sc in last st. Stitch count: (87, 95, 103)

Row 18: Ch-1, turn, sk first 2 sts, * (sc, dc) in next, sk next st * repeat between * * (41, 45, 49) more times. Sc in last st. Stitch count: (85, 93, 101)

Continue decreasing until you reach row (43, 45, 47) ending with (35, 39, 43) sts. Do not fasten off.

Turn work clockwise to add finishing edge. Sc in each st/row end around the entire dog sweater, placing 3 scs in each corner. Fasten off using Invisible Join.

Sew buttons onto chest flap, making sure they line up with the buttonholes. You're done!

Materials:

- Bernat Super Value (5 oz / 140 g)

Sizes S (M-L-XL)
Main Color (MC) 1 (1-1-1) ball
Contrast A 1 (1-1-1) ball
Contrast B 1 (1-1-1) ball
Contrast C 1 (1-1-1) ball
Contrast D 1 (1-1-1) ball
Contrast E 1 (1-1-1) ball

- Sizes 4 mm (US F) and 4.5 mm (US G) crochet hook or size needed to obtain gauge.
- **Gauge 14 dc and 8 rows = 4 ins [10 cm] with larger hook.**

Size

- Small 10 ins [25.5 cm]
- Medium 16 ins [40.5 cm]
- Large 24 ins [61 cm]
- XL 30 ins [76 cm]

Instructions

Stripe Pat:

1 row A, 1 row B, 1 row C, 1 row D, 1 row E and 1 row MC. Rep last 6 rows for stripe pat throughout.

Neck Ribbing:

With MC and smaller hook, ch 8 loosely.

1st row: 1 sc in 2nd ch from hook. 1 sc in each ch to end of ch. Ch 1. Turn.

2nd row: Working in back loop only of each st, work 1 sc in each st to end of row. Ch 1. Turn. Rep last row 30 (46-70-82) times more omitting turning ch at end of last row.

Body:

Change to larger hook.
1st row: (RS). Ch 3 (counts as first dc). Work a further 33 (49-73-85) dc across long edge of neck ribbing. 34 (50-74-86) dc. Join A. Ch 3. Turn. Cont in stripe pat as follows:
2nd row: 1 dc in first dc – inc made. 1 dc in each dc to last dc. 2 dc in last dc – inc made. Ch 3. Turn. Rep last row 2 (6-10-16) times more. 40 (64-96-120) dc.

Shape Leg Opening:

- **First Side:**

Next row: Miss first dc. 1 dc in each of next 4 (7-11-15) dc. 5 (8-12-16) dc. Ch 3. Turn. Leave rem sts unworked.
Next row: Miss first dc. 1 dc in next dc and each dc to end of row. Ch 3. Turn. Rep last row 1 (3-5-5) time(s) more omitting turning ch at end of last row. Fasten off.

- **Center Section:**

Next row: With RS facing, miss next 4 (7-9-12) dc, join yarn with ss in next dc. Ch 3. 1 dc in each of next 21 (33-53-63) dc. 22 (34-54-64) dc. Ch 3. Turn. Leave rem sts unworked.
Next row: Miss first dc. 1 dc in next dc and each dc to end of row. Ch 3. Turn. Rep last row 1 (3-5-5) time(s) more omitting turning ch at end of last row. Fasten off.

- **Second Side:**

Next row: With RS facing miss next 4 (7-9-12) unworked dc, join yarn with ss in next dc. Ch 3. 1 dc in each of next 4 (7-9-12) dc. 5 (8-10-13) dc. Ch 3. Turn.
Next row: Miss first dc. 1 dc in next dc and each dc to end of row.
Ch 3. Turn. Rep last row 1 (3-5-5) time(s). Joining Row: Miss first dc. 1 dc in next dc and each dc across Second Side. Ch 4 (7-9-12) loosely. 1 dc in each dc across Center Section. Ch 4 (7-9-12) loosely. 1 dc in each dc across First Side. Ch 3. Turn.

Next row: Miss first dc. 1 dc in each of next 4 (7-9-12) dc. 1 dc in each of next 4 (7-9-12) ch. 1 dc in each of next 22 (34-54-64) dc. 1 dc in each of next 4 (7-9-12) ch. 1 dc in each of next 5 (8-10-13) dc. 40 (64-96- 120) dc. Ch 3. Turn.

Next row: Miss first dc. 1 dc in next dc and each dc across. Ch 3. Turn. Rep last row until work from Joining Row meas ures approx 4½ (7-10½-11½) ins [11.5 (18- 26.5-29) cm] ending with RS facing for next row and omitting turning ch at end of last row.

Shape Belly:

Next row: Ss in each of first 7 (10-15-19) dc. Ch 3. 1 dc in each of next 27 (45-67-83) dc. Ch 3. Turn. Leave rem sts unworked. 28 (46-68-84) dc.

Next row: Miss first dc. (Yoh and draw up a loop in next st. Yoh and draw through 2 loops on hook) twice. Yoh and draw through all loops on hook - dc2tog made. 1 dc in next dc and each dc to last 3 dc. Dc2tog over next 2 dc. 1 dc in last dc. Ch 3. Turn. Rep last row 3 (6-9-11) times more. 20 (32-48- 60) dc.

Cont even until work from 1st row after Neck Ribbing measures 10½ (16-22-25) ins [26.5 (40.5-56-63.5) cm] omitting turning ch at end of last row. Fasten off. Sew seam from Neck Ribbing to Belly shaping.

Back Edging:

With RS facing, MC and larger hook, join yarn with ss at seam. Ch 1. Work 1 row sc evenly around Belly shaping and back edge, working 3 sc in corners. Join with ss to first sc. Fasten off.

Leg Edging:

With RS facing, MC and larger hook, join yarn with ss in any st of Leg Opening. Ch 1. Work 1 row sc evenly around Leg Opening. Join with ss to first sc. Fasten off.

Leg Bands:

- With MC, ch 6 loosely.

1st row: 1 sc in 2nd ch from hook. 1 sc in each ch to end of ch. Ch 1. Turn.

2nd row: Working in back loop only of each st, work 1 sc in each st to end of row. Ch 1. Turn. Rep last row until work from beg measures 5 (6-8-9½) ins [12.5 (15- 20.5-24) cm]. Fasten off. Sew leg band seam. Sew leg band to leg edging.

Houndstooth Dog Sweater

Materials:

- Red Heart® Comfort® (16 oz/454 g; 867 yds/792 m)

Sizes

Contrast A Cream Fleck (5100) 1 1 2 ball(s)

Contrast B Gray (3150) 1 1 2 ball(s)

- Size U.S. I/9 (5.5 mm) crochet hook or size needed to obtain gauge.
- Yarn needle.
- **Gauge 12 sts and 16 rows = 4" [10 cm] in pat.**

Size

- S 10" [25.5 cm]
- M 13" [33 cm]
- L 16" [40.5 cm]

Pattern notes:

- The instructions are written for smallest size. If changes are necessary for larger sizes the instructions will be written thus ( ). Numbers for each size are shown in the same color throughout the pattern. When only one number is given in black, it applies to all sizes.
- **Note**: To change color, pat to last 2 loops on hook and draw new color through last 2 loops, then proceed in new color

Instructions

Body Pat:

1st row: (WS). With B, ch 1. 1 sc in rst sc. *Lsc over next sc. 1 sc in next sc. Rep from * to end of row. Turn.

2nd row: Ch 1. 1 sc in each st to end of row. Join A. Turn.

3rd and 4th rows: With A, as 1st and 2nd rows. Join B at end of last row. These 4 rows form Body Pat.

Dog Coat:

Neckband: With B, ch 6.

1st row: (RS). 1 sc in 2nd ch from hook and in each ch to end of chain. Turn. 5 sts.

2nd row: Ch 1. 1 scbl in each st to end of row. Turn. Rep 2nd row until 29 (39-49) rows have been worked. Do not fasten off

Body

1st row: (RS). Ch 1. Turn work sideways. Work 29 (39-49) sc evenly across long edge of Neckband. Turn. 29 (39-49) sc.

2nd row: Ch 1. 1 (2-1) sc in rst sc. *2 sc in next sc. 1 sc in next sc. Rep from * to end of row. 43 (59-73) sc.

3rd row: Ch 1. 1 sc in each sc to end of row. Join B. Turn

Work 2 rows in Body Pat.

Divide for Leg Openings:

1st row: (WS): Keeping cont of Body Pat, pat across rst 5 (7-9) sts. Turn. Leave rem sts unworked. Work 9 (13-17) rows even in pat across 5 (7-9) sts. Fasten off.

With WS facing, skip next 3 (5-7) sts of last long row for leg opening. Join corresponding color with sl st to next st. Ch 1. Work 10 (14-18) rows in pat across next 27 (35-41) sts for Back. Fasten off.

With WS facing, skip next 3 (5-7) sts of last long row for 2nd leg opening. Join corresponding color with sl st to next st. Ch 1. Work 10 (14-18) rows in pat across last 5 (7-9) sts. Do not fasten off. **Joining row: (WS).** Pat across rst 5 (7-9) sts. Ch 3 (5-7). Pat across next 27 (35-41) sts. Ch 3 (5-7). Pat across last 5 (7-9) sts. Turn.

Next row: Ch 1. Pat across rst 5 (7-9) sts. 1 sc in each of next 3 (5-7) ch. Pat across next 27 (35-41) sts. 1 sc in each of next 3 (5-7) ch. Pat across last 5 (7-9) sts. Turn. 43 (59-73) sts.

Work 1 row even in pat.

Shape Back: Keeping cont of pat, proceed as follows:

1st row: (RS). Ch 1. Sc2tog. Pat to last 2 sts. Sc2tog. Turn.

2nd row: Work even in pat. Rep last 2 rows 13 times more. 15 (31-45) sts rem. Fasten off.

Edging for Leg Openings

1st rnd: (RS). Join B with sl st in any st at leg opening. Ch 1. 1 sc in same sp as sl st. Work a futher 23 (35-50) sc evenly around. Join with sl st to rst sc. 24 (36-51) sc.

2nd rnd: Ch 1. *Sc2tog. 1 sc in next st. Rep from * around. Join with sl st to rst st. 16 (24-34) sts.

3rd rnd: Ch 1. 1 sc in each st around. Join with sl st to rst st.

4th rnd: Ch 1. 1 sc in first sc. *Sc2tog. 1 sc in next st. Rep from * to last 0 (2-0) sc. (Sc2tog) 0 (1-0) time. Join with sl st to rst st. 11 (16-23) sts.

5th rnd: As 3rd rnd.

6th rnd: Ch 1. Working from left to right, instead of from right to left, as usual, work 1 reverse sc in each sc around. Join with sl st to rst sc. Fasten off.

Finishing

Sew underbody seam from Neckband to rst shaping row of Back.

- **Edging**:

1st rnd: (RS). Join B with sl st at seam. Ch 1. Work sc evenly around entire edge working 3 sc in corners. Join with sl st to rst sc.

2nd rnd: Working from left to right, instead of from right to left, as usual, work 1 reverse sc in each sc around. Join with sl st to rst sc. Fasten off.

Fab Dog Coat

Materials:

- Bernat® Super Value™ (7 oz/197 g; 440 yds/402 m)

Sizes S M L XL

Berry (00607) 1 1 2 2 ball(s)

- Size U.S. H/8 (5 mm) crochet hook or size needed to obtain gauge
- **Gauge 7 sts and 6 rows = 4" [10 cm] in pat**

Size

- S 10" [25.5 cm]
- M 13" [33 cm]
- L 16" [40.5 cm]
- XL 24" [61 cm]

Pattern notes:

- The instructions are written for smallest size. If changes are necessary for larger size the instructions will be written thus ( ). Ch 34 (38-48-64) loosely.

Instructions

1st row: (RS). 1 sc in 2nd ch from hook. 1 sc in each ch across. 33 (37-47-63) sts. Turn.

2nd row: Ch 1. 1 sc in each sc to end of row. Turn. Proceed in pat as follows. 1st row: (RS). Ch 1. 1 sc in first st. *1 dc in next st. 1 sc in next st. Rep from * to end of row. Turn. 2nd row: Ch 3 (counts as dc). *1 sc in next dc. 1 dc in next sc. Rep from* to end of row. Turn. **3rd row:** Ch 1. 2 sc in first dc (Inc made). *1 dc in next sc. 1 sc in next dc. Rep from * to last 2 sts. 1 dc in next sc. 2 sc in last dc (Inc made). Turn.

4th row: Ch 3 (counts as dc). 1 dc in first sc (inc made). *1 dc in next sc. 1 sc in next dc. Rep from * to last 2 sts. 1 dc in next sc. 2 dc in last sc (inc made). Turn.

5th row: Ch 1. 2 sc in first dc (Inc made). 1 dc in next dc. *1 sc in next dc. 1 dc in next sc. Rep from * to last 3 sts. 1 sc in next dc. 1 dc in next dc. 2 sc in last dc (inc made). Turn. Rep 4th and 5th rows 0 (1-2-4) time(s) more, then rep 4th row 0 (1-0-1) time more. 39 (49-61-87) sts. Work 1 (0-1-0) row even in pat.

Leg Openings:

Next row: (RS). Pat across 3 (5-7-9) sts. Sl st across next 5 (5-5-7) sts. Ch 1. Pat across 23 (29-37-55) sts. Sl st across next 5 (5-5-7) sts. Pat to end of row.

Note: All Leg sections are worked at the same time using separate balls of yarn for each section. Work 1 (1½-1½-2½)" [2.5 (4-4-6) cm] in pat, ending with RS row.

Joining row: (WS). Pat across 3 (5-7-9) sts. Ch 5 (5-5-7). Pat across 23 (29-37-55) sts. Ch 5 (5-5-7). Pat to end of row.

Next row: Pat across 3 (5-7-9) sts. Pat across next 5 (5-5-7) ch. Pat across 23 (29-37-55) sts. Pat across next 5 (5-5-7) ch. Pat to end of row. 39 (49-61-87) sts.

Continue even in pat until work after neckband measures 5 (6½- 8-11)" [12.5 (16.5-20.5-28) cm], ending with WS row. Place marker at each end of last row.

Back Shaping:

Next row: Sl st across first 4 (5-6- 9) sts. Ch 1. Pat to last 4 (5-6-9) sts. Turn. Leave rem sts unworked. 31 (39-49-69) sts.

Next row: Ch 1. Draw up a loop in each of first 2 sts. Yoh and draw through all loops on hook – sc2tog made. Pat to last 2 sts. Sc2tog over last 2 sts. Turn. Rep last row 5 (5-8-9) times more. 19 (27-31-49) sts rem. Continue even in pat until work after neckband measures 10 (12½- 15½-21)" [25.5 (32-39.5-53.5) cm], ending with WS row. Fasten off.

Back Edging

1st row: (RS). Join yarn with sl st at marker. Ch 1. Work sc evenly across back edge to opposite marker. Turn.

2nd row: Ch 1. 1 sc in each sc across. Fasten off. Sew neck and belly seam.

Leg Edging

1st rnd: (RS). Join yarn with sl st at leg opening. Ch 1. Work sc evenly around. Join with sl st to first sc.

2nd rnd: Ch 1. 1 sc in each sc around. Join with sl st to first sc. Fasten off.

Beginner Dog Coat

Materials:

- Caron® Kindness™ (7 oz/198 g; 345 yds/315 m)
Tomato (53010) 2 3 4 5 balls
- Size U.S. H/8 (5 mm) crochet hook or size needed to obtain gauge. Stitch markers
- **Gauge** 13 sc and 14 rows = 4" [10 cm]

Size

- S 10" [25.5 cm]
- M 13" [33 cm]
- L 16" [40.5 cm]
- XL 24" [61 cm]

Pattern notes:

- The instructions are written for smallest size. If changes are necessary for larger size the instructions will be written thus ( ).

Instructions

Ch 34 (38-48-64) loosely.

1st row: (RS). 1 sc in 2nd ch from hook. 1 sc in each ch to end of chain. 33 (37-47-63) sc. Turn.

2nd row: Ch 1. 1 sc in each sc to end of row. Turn.

Proceed in pat as follows.

1st row: (RS). Ch 1. 1 sc in first st. *1 dc in next st. 1 sc in next st. Rep from * to end of row. Turn.

2nd row: Ch 3 (counts as dc). *1 sc in next dc. 1 dc in next sc. Rep from* to end of row. Turn. Last 2 rows form pat.

3rd row: Ch 1. 2 sc in first dc (inc made). *1 dc in next sc. 1 sc in next dc. Rep from * to last 2 sts. 1 dc in next sc. 2 sc in last dc (inc made). Turn.

4th row: Ch 3 (counts as dc). 1 dc in first sc (inc made). *1 dc in next sc. 1 sc in next dc. Rep from * to last 2 sts. 1 dc in next sc. 2 dc in last sc (inc made). Turn.

5th row: Ch 1. 2 sc in first dc (inc made). 1 dc in next dc. *1 sc in next dc. 1 dc in next sc. Rep from * to last 3 sts. 1 sc in next dc. 1 dc in next dc. 2 sc in last dc (inc made). Turn. Rep 4th and 5th rows 0 (1-2-4) time(s) more, then 4th row 0 (1- 0-1) time more. 39 (49-61-87) sts. Work 1 (0-1-0) row even in pat.

Leg Openings:

Next row: (RS). Pat across 3 (5- 7-9) sts. Sl st in each of next 5 (5-5-7) sts. Pat across 23 (29-37- 55) sts. Sl st in each of next 5 (5- 5-7) sts. Pat to end of row. Turn.

Note: All Leg sections are worked at the same time using separate balls of yarn for each section. Work 1 (1½-1½-2½)" [2.5 (4- 4-6) cm] in pat, ending with RS row.

Joining row: (WS). Pat across 3 (5-7-9) sts. Ch 5 (5-5-7). Pat across 23 (29-37-55) sts. Ch 5 (5- 5-7). Pat to end of row. Turn.

Next row: Pat across 3 (5-7-9) sts. Pat across next 5 (5-5-7) ch. Pat across 23 (29-37-55) sts. Pat across next 5 (5-5-7) ch. Pat to end of row. 39 (49-61-87) sts. Turn.

Cont even in pat until work after neckband measures 5 (6½-8-11)" [12.5 (16.5-20.5-28) cm], ending on a WS row. PM at each end of last row.

Back Shaping:

Next row: Sl st in each of first 4 (5-6-9) sts. Pat to last 4 (5-6-9) sts. Turn. Leave rem sts unworked. 31 (39- 49-69) sts rem.

Next row: Ch 1. Sc2tog. Pat to last 2 sts. Sc2tog. Turn. Rep last row 5 (5-8-9) times more. 19 (27-31-49) sts rem. Cont even in pat until work after neckband measures 10 (12½-15½-21)" [25.5 (32- 39.5-53.5) cm], ending on a WS row. Fasten off.

Back Edging

1st row: (RS). Join yarn with sl st at marker. Ch 1. Work sc evenly across back edge to opposite marker. Turn.

2nd row: Ch 1. 1 sc in each sc to end of row. Fasten off.

Finishing

Sew neck and belly seam.

- **Leg Edging:**

1st rnd: (RS). Join yarn with sl st at leg opening. Ch 1. Work sc evenly around. Join with sl st to first sc.

2nd rnd: Ch 1. 1 sc in each sc around. Join with sl st to first sc. Fasten off.

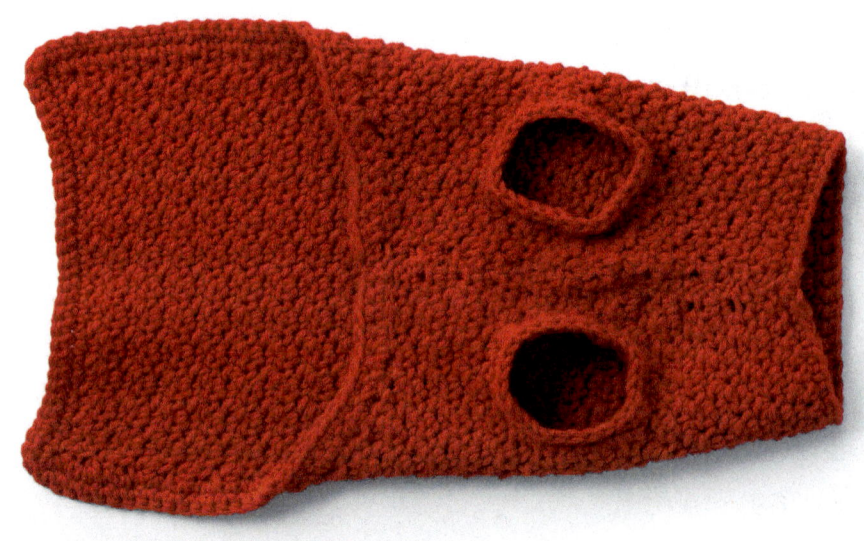

Materials:

- RED HEART® "Soft Yarn™":

1 (2, 2) Balls No. 4614 Black CA;

1 ball each No. 9114 Honey CB, No. 9779 Berry CC, No. 9522 Leaf CD, No. 4422 Tangerine CE, No. 9518 Teal CF, No. 9520 Seafoam CG, No. 4601 Off White CH, No. 6768 Pink CI, and No. 3729 Grape CJ [solid colors – 5 oz (140 g), 256 yd (234 m); print colors – 4 oz (113 g), 204 yd (187 m)].

- Crochet Hook: 5mm [US H-8].
- Yarn needle; one 3/4" button.
- **GAUGE: Square = 4.5" x 4.5".**

Size

To Fit Chest: 19 (23, 28)".
To Fit Neck: 16 (18, 20)".
To Fit Length: 10 (12, 16)".

Pattern notes:

Directions are for size small; changes for medium and large are in parentheses

Instructions

BASIC GRANNY SQUARE (See color sequence below):

Ch 6; join with a sl st to form a ring.

Rnd 1: Ch 5 (counts as dc, ch 2), [3 dc in ring, ch 2] 3 times, 2 dc in ring; join with a sl st in 3rd ch of ch-5. Fasten off.

Rnd 2: Join yarn in any ch-2 sp; ch 5, 3 dc in same sp, [ch 1, (3 dc, ch 2, 3 dc) all in next sp] 3 times, ch 1, 2 dc in beg sp; join. Fasten off.

Rnd 3: Join yarn in any ch-2 sp; ch 5, 3 dc in same sp, * ch 1, 3 dc in next ch-1 sp, ch 1 **, (3 dc, ch 2, 3 dc) all in corner ch-2 sp; rep from * around, end at **; 2 dc in beg sp; join. Fasten off.

Rnd 4: Join yarn in any ch-2 sp; ch 5, 3 dc in same sp, * [ch 1, 3 dc in next sp] twice, ch 1 **, (3 dc, ch 2, 3 dc) all in corner ch-2 sp; rep from * around, end at **; 2 dc in beg sp; join Fasten off.

Make 2 (3, 4) squares in the following color sequence:
Rnd 1: CB; Rnd 2: CC; Rnd 3: CD; Rnd 4: CA.
Make 2 (3, 4) squares in the following color sequence:
Rnd 1: CE; Rnd 2: CF; Rnd 3: CG; Rnd 4: CA.
Make 2 (3, 4) squares in the following color sequence:
Rnd 1: CH; Rnd 2: CI; Rnd 3: CJ; Rnd 4: CA

BODY

Sew 6 (9, 12) squares together. Weave in ends.
Neck: Sew one square on each side of body. Make a chain 20 (25, 30)" long and weave in and out of granny squares for neck closure

CHEST PANEL

Size Small: Make 1 square in colors of your choice.
Row 5: Join yarn in any corner sp; ch 3, 2 dc in same sp, [ch 1, 3 dc in ch-1 sp] 3 times, ch 1, 3 dc in next corner sp. Fasten off. Weave in ends

Sizes Medium and Large: Make 1 square in colors of your choice.

Rnd 5: Join yarn in any ch-2 sp; ch 5, 3 dc in same sp, [ch 1, 3 dc in next sp] 3 times, ch 1 **, (3 dc, ch 2, 3 dc) all in next corner sp; rep from * around, end at **; 2 dc in beg sp; join. Fasten off.

Rnd 6: Join yarn in any ch-2 sp; ch 5, 3 dc in same sp, [ch 1, 3 dc in next sp] 4 times, ch 1 **, (3 dc, ch 2, 3 dc) all in next corner sp; rep from * around, end at **; 2 dc in beg sp; join. Fasten off.

Row 7: Join yarn in any ch-2 sp; ch 3, 2 dc in same sp, [ch 1, 3 dc in ch-1 sp] 5 times, ch 1, 3 dc in next corner sp. Fasten off. Weave in ends

FINISHING:

Sew the chest panel to both sides of the body. Sew on one button at the neck for closure, using a ch-1 sp as the buttonhole. Weave in ends

Textured Dog Coat

Materials:

- Caron® Cakes™ (7.1 oz/200 g; 383 yds/350 m)

Sizes S M L XL

Turkish Delight (17037) or Honey Berry (17044) 1 1 2 2 balls

- Sizes U.S. G/6 (4 mm) and U.S. 7 (4.5 mm) crochet hooks or size needed to obtain gauge
- **GAUGE 14 sc and 15 rows = 4" [10 cm] with larger hook**

Size

- S 10" [25.5 cm]
- M 16" [40.5 cm]
- L 24" [61 cm]
- XL 30" [76 cm

Pattern notes:

- The instructions are written for smallest size. If changes are necessary for larger size the instructions will be written thus ( ).

Instructions

Neck Ribbing:

With smaller hook, ch 17 (21-25-31) loosely.

1st row: 1 sc in 2nd ch from hook. 1 sc in each ch to end of chain. Turn. 16 (20-24-30) sc.

2nd row: Ch 1. Working in back loops only, work 1 sc in each st to end of row. Turn. Rep last row 30 (46-70-82) times more.

Body

Change to larger hook.

1st row: (RS). Ch 1. Work 34 (50- 74-86) sc across long edge of neck ribbing. Turn.

2nd row: Ch 3 (counts as dc). *1 sc in next st. 1 dc in next st. Rep from * to last st. 1 sc in last st.

3rd row: Ch 1. (1 sc. 1 dc) in first sc (inc made). *1 sc in next dc. 1 dc in next sc. Rep from * ending with (1 sc. 1 dc) in top of turning ch 3 (inc made). Turn.

4th row: Ch 3 (counts as dc). 1 sc in first dc (inc made). *1 dc in next sc. 1 sc in next dc. Rep from * ending with (1 dc. 1 sc) in last sc (inc made). Turn.

Rep last 2 rows 1 (3-4-8) time(s) more. 42 (66-94-122) sts

Shape Leg Opening:

First Side:

Next row: Ch 3 (counts as dc). Pat across next 5 (7-11-17) sts. Turn.

Leave rem sts unworked.

Work 3 (3-5-7) rows even in pat over these 6 (8-12-18) sts. Fasten off

Center Section:

Next row: (RS). Skip next 4 (8-10-12) sts. Join yarn with sl st in next st. Ch 3 (counts as dc). Pat across next 21 (33-49-61) sts. Turn.

Leave rem sts unworked.

Work 3 (3-5-7) rows even in pat over these 22 (34-50-62) sts. Fasten off.

Second Side:

Next row: (RS). Skip next 4 (8-10-12) sts. Join yarn with sl st in next st. Ch 3 (counts as dc). Pat across next 5 (7-11- 17) sts. Turn

Work 3 (3-5-7) rows even in pat over these 6 (8-12-18) sts. Do not fasten off.

Joining Row: (RS). Ch 3 (counts as dc). Pat across next 5 (7-11-17) sts of Second Side. Ch 4 (8-10-12) loosely. Pat across 22 (34-50-62) sts of Center Section. Ch 4 (8-10-12) loosely. Pat across 6 (8-12-18) sts of First Side. Turn.

Next row: Ch 3 (counts as dc). Pat across next 5 (7-11-17) sts. Pat across next 4 (8-10-12) ch. Pat across next 22 (34-50-62) sts. Pat across next 4 (8-10-12) ch. Pat to end of row. Turn. 42 (66-94-122) sts.

Work even in pat until work from Joining Row measures approx 5 (7-10½-12)" [12.5 (18-26.5-30.5) cm], ending on a WS row.

Shape Belly:

Next row: Sl st in each of first 7 (11-15-19) sts. Ch 3 (counts as dc). Pat across next 29 (45-65-85) sts. Turn. Leave rem sts unworked. 30 (46-66-86) sts.

Next row: Ch 2 (does not count as st). hdc2tog over first 2 sts. Pat to last 2 sts. hdc2tog over last 2 sts. Turn.

Rep last row 4 (5-8-12) times more. 20 (34-48-60) sts.

Cont even in pat until work from 1st row after Neck Ribbing measures 10½ (16-21-24)" [26.5(40.5-53.5-61) cm]. Fasten off.

Sew seam from Neck Ribbing to Belly shaping.

Back Edging:

(RS). Join yarn with sl st at seam. With larger hook, ch 1. Work 1 row sc evenly around Belly shaping and back edge, working 3 sc in corners. Join with sl st to first sc. Fasten off.

Leg Edging:

(RS). Join yarn with sl st in any st of Leg Opening. With larger hook, ch 1. Work 1 row sc evenly around Leg Opening. Join with sl st to first sc. Fasten off.

Leg Bands (make 2):

With smaller hook, ch 6 (6-8-8) loosely.

1st row: 1 sc in 2nd ch from hook. 1 sc in each ch to end of chain. Turn. 5 (5-7-7) sc.

2nd row: Ch 1. Working in back loops only, work 1 sc in each st to end of row. Turn. Rep last row until work (when slightly stretched) measures length to fit around Leg Edging. Fasten off.

Sew Leg Band seam. Sew side of Leg Band to Leg Edging.

Fold Neck Ribbing in half to WS and sew side edge loosely in position

Purpleicious Dog Coat

Materials:

- RED HEART® "Super Saver®": 1 skein 528 Medium Purple A.
- RED HEART® "Pomp-a-Doodle™": 1 ball 9540 Purple Passion B.
- Crochet Hooks: 4mm [US G-6] and 5.5mm [US I-9].
- Yarn needle, 3 split-lock stitch markers, three 5/8" buttons, hand sewing thread and needle, 14" of 5/8""-wide white satin ribbon.
- **GAUGE: 10 sts = 4" in pattern with A and larger hook.**

Size

- Length: 13½ (16½, 19½)".
- Chest: 16 (20, 24)"

Pattern notes:

- Directions are for Size Small; changes for Medium and Large are in parentheses.

Instructions

COAT

Row 1 (Right Side): With larger hook and A, ch 41 (51, 61), sc in 2nd ch from hook, dc in next ch, * sc in next ch, dc in next ch; repeat from * across; turn – 40 (50, 60) sts.

Row 2: Ch 1, * sc in dc, dc in sc; repeat from * across; turn. Repeat Row 2 for pattern until 9 (12, 14)" from beginning, end by working a wrong side row.

Divide for Back and Fronts-Right Front
Keeping continuity of pattern, work across first 8 (10, 12) sts; turn. Work even in pattern on these sts until armhole depth is 4 (4, 5)". Fasten off.

Back
With right side facing, join yarn in next st of last long row; work pattern in same st and next 23 (29, 35) sts; turn – 24 (30, 36) sts. Work even until back is same length as front. Fasten off.

Left Front
With right side facing, join yarn in next st of last long row; work pattern across last 8 (10, 12) sts; turn. Work even in pattern until same length as front. Fasten off.

Edging
Row 1: With right side facing, join A at top of Left Front; ch 1, work 35 (45, 55) sc to bottom corner, 3 sc in corner, 38 (48, 58) sc to next corner, 3 sc in corner, 35 (45, 55) sc to top of Right Front; turn. Place 3 evenly spaced markers on Right Front for button holes.
Row 2: Ch 1, [sc to marker, ch 2, skip next 2 sc] 3 times, sc in each sc around and 3 sc in corner sc; turn.
Row 3: Ch 1, sc in each sc around and 2 sc in each ch-2 space and 3 sc in each corner sc. Fasten off

Neck & Ties
Row 1: With right side facing and smaller hook, join A in top of Left Front Edging; ch 35. Fasten off.
Chain 36, sc in 2nd ch from hook and in each ch to end, work 10 (12, 14) sc across Right Front, 26 (32, 38) sc across Back, 10 (12, 14) sc across Left Front and 35 sc across ch. Fasten off.

Row 2: With wrong side facing, skip first 35 sc for tie, sc in next 46 (56, 66) sc, leaving last 35 sc free for tie; turn.

Row 3: Ch 1, sc in each sc across. Fasten off.

Sleeves

Round 1: With right side facing and larger hook, join A at center of underarm; ch 1, work 21 (21, 25) sc around armhole; join.

Rounds 2-4 (2-6, 2-8): Ch 1, sc in each sc around; join.

Finish off at end of last round.

Collar

NOTE: Be careful not to pull pom poms through stitches.

At beginning of each row, ch 2 instead of ch 1 to maintain placement of pom poms.

Row 1: With right side facing and larger hook, join B in first sc of Neck; ch 1, (working in yarn between pom poms throughout), sc in each sc across; turn.

Rows 2-7 (2-9, 2-11): Ch 2, sc in each sc across; turn.

Fasten off at end of last row.

Finishing

Sew on buttons opposite button holes. Use crochet hook to pull ribbon through center back of coat below collar as in photo. Tie into bow

Printed in Dunstable, United Kingdom